THE
VISION GUIDED
LIFE

God's Strategy for Fulfilling Your Destiny

KAY AND OLU TAIWO

THE VISION GUIDED LIFE

The Vision Guided Life: God's Strategy for Fulfilling Your Destiny

ISBN 978-0-9676572-8-8 Second Edition

ISBN 978-0-9676572-3-3 First Edition

Copyright © 2014 by Vision for Maximum Impact, LLC. Kayode & Olumide Taiwo

P.O. Box 3553, Broken Arrow, OK 74013, USA. Published by Vision for Maximum Impact, LLC.

Second Edition.

Contents

What People Are Saying About *The Vision Guided Life*

"Kay and Olu introduce this outstanding book with a chapter on the Power of Vision, then they follow by looking at 8 things that Vision is not. The rest of the book is dedicated to looking at what Vision is. Your understanding of your Life Purpose and Passion will deepen and expand as you read this book and discover why you need more than Purpose - You need a Vision also. Capture a true understanding of God's Vision for your life and you will become unstoppable!...This is a powerful book that if you really follow and put into action in your life, will transform your life. It certainly has my full recommendations."
— *Pamela Jill Rapley*

"...Kay and Olu do not stop at merely defining vision, but take it a step further into making application to our lives. There are fitting anecdotes throughout the book to help the reader understand the principles and concepts on a deeper level. They have also included case studies and a 28-day group exercise in order to help readers focus on their vision and discover how it unlocks the secrets to God's destiny for their lives."
— *Bil Howard for Readers' Favorite*

"My favorite tool is a pink highlighter, which is now the color of a good portion of the text. Vision Guided Life gets a spot on my fav book/important reference bookcase for easy access (I have several bookcases categorized based on importance/relevance of material.) Thank you for taking the time to share what you've learned in your book. What a gift!" — *Leanne Canady*

"This ...book takes all the other books I've read on setting up vision statements and missions statements and all of that and puts it into a Biblical framework. Like what God's vision statement is. And how His vision statement is the template for our own vision statement. Tons of little tidbits of information that I'll re-read later. Yes, vision is important. They tell why, and they tell how." — *G. Older*

Introduction

The vivid need for this book became apparent on our trip to South Africa and Zimbabwe some years ago. In South Africa, we conducted meetings in Johannesburg, Cape Town, and Durban.

While speaking at a packed conference in the beautiful city of Johannesburg we conducted a session on the subject of vision. After the meeting, the response was remarkable; particularly from the leaders present. In the audience was the Secretary General of the Assemblies of God. He said to us very emphatically, "what was shared here needs to be heard by those in government."

The importance of the subject of vision applies to the individual, family, business, Church, and a nation.

Its importance becomes obvious where it is lacking. It is the nature of vision to restore what was destroyed or damaged.

In the book of beginnings, Genesis, chapter 1, the first scenario is one of chaos. The Bible tells us that the earth was without form, and void. Then God began to move in the situation, and He transformed it. That's the nature of God – to correct by putting things back in order.

The whole earth is crying for the manifestation of the sons of God. But the question is, will the sons and daughters of God take their place and align with His purpose to see the Kingdom of God expanded?

Africa is not a poor continent. It is a very rich continent.

In fact, arguably, Africa is richer in natural resources than many of the so-called first world nations. However, there has been gross mismanagement in many cases, because leaders without vision are ruling. The Bible says that when the blind lead the blind, both will fall into a ditch (Matthew 15:14). It is time for men and women with divine insight to take their place and be the change agents the world is desperately looking for.

Destiny Zone

What is the "destiny zone"? The "destiny zone" is where your God-given vision, identity, and purpose are perfectly synchronized with one another. In fact, we conduct what we term, 'VIP Seminars.' The acronym VIP stands for: Vision, Identity and Purpose. These seminars effectively show how these three subjects connect with each other.

In this diagram, notice what completes the cycle: We have vision, identity, and purpose.

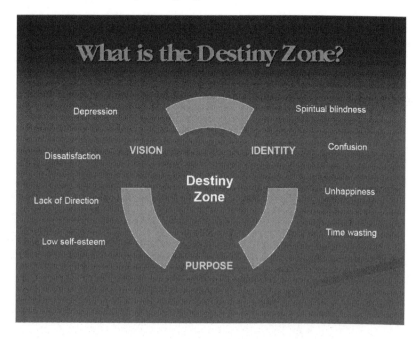

As a ministry, this is what we key on; that is, to extend the Kingdom of God to individuals by helping the Body of Christ realize that each person possesses a God-given vision to positively impact his or her world. This vision aligned with who we are in Christ helps us to fulfill our purpose on this planet.

In other words, when I have a clear mandate from God, I see clearly from His vantage point. When I understand who I am in the context of His purpose, there is a synergy that takes place. The cycle is complete.

Outside the Destiny Zone

But now, let's look at what happens outside of the destiny zone cycle. What happens when I'm not within the scope of God's vision for my life, when I haven't fully grasped who I am in relation to that vision, and when I have a lack of purpose?

There is a sense of depression and deep dissatisfaction. Outside the destiny zone, life becomes a series of experiments. It is amazing that even in the church, far too many people live outside of the destiny zone.

Many years ago we received a letter from London, England. The writer was a lady who read our book, Uncovering the Hidden Stranger Within: Answering the Question of Identity. Below is an excerpt of the letter:

> *Your book put all my spiritual anxieties into perspective. Due to the enormous suffering, rejection, condemnation, and ridicule I encountered, I was a little dizzy by what was actually happening to me. But 1 Peter 4:12 explains it, and your book has illuminated everything for me. I can now start to enjoy my walk in the Lord with security and confidence.*

When you don't know your purpose, there's a lack of direction and you waste a lot of time. When purpose is not known, a person either becomes complacent about life or pursues an unhealthy obsession. Notice this woman's words: "I can now start to enjoy my walk in the Lord with security and confidence." Let's put this in context, using the following illustration:

> *"When purpose is not known, a person either becomes complacent about life or pursues an unhealthy obsession."*

If you are listening to a message on a CD, the phone rings, or someone comes to your door, you put the message on pause to attend to the phone or to respond to the person at the door. This means that your knowledge of the contents of the CD was paused, and you do not know the beneficial instruction that follows. The only way to get the required information is to go back to the device and click on play. In the context of life, for many this 'interruption' could last ten seconds or ten years. Some have last 'played out' their purpose decades ago and have been living perpetually in 'pause' mode ever since. Tragic indeed.

In some subtle sense, in life many of us start our journey on track, but because of the distractions that we are faced with, "life" is put on pause as we attend to other things. It is only when we realign ourselves to our God-given destiny and obtain the next instruction that God has for us that we go to the next level.

How can we assess if we are doing well or not if we are not getting the instruction or having a clear sense of direction? That is where vision comes in. Vision is seeing what God wants us to do in the big picture and taking steps towards making that picture a reality.

For instance, when God spoke to Moses, He told him that he was going to set His people free and take them to a promised land. However, in going through that process, Moses had to become what God wanted him to be. He had to be focused. He had to know God's plan clearly so that when he faced resistance from Pharaoh, he could still maintain his sense of direction. He held on because he had a clear sense of direction.

The lady who wrote us concluded, "I can now start to enjoy my walk in the Lord with security and confidence." Think about this statement.

In your own personal life, are you moving in God's direction for your life; or is your life in a state of perpetual pause? That's an important question to answer. Our prayer is that your questions will be answered in this book, *The Vision Guided Life*.

SECTION I:
THE IMPACT OF VISION

CHAPTER 1

THE POWER OF VISION

Robert Woodruff, who was the President of Coca Cola, from 1923 to 1955, a 32-year span, cast the following vision for Coca Cola. Right after World War II, he said, "In my lifetime I want everyone in the world to have tasted Coke."

— John Maxwell[1]

Do you not know that those who run in a race all run, but one receives the prize? Run in such a way that you may obtain it. And everyone who competes for the prize is temperate in all things. Now they do it to obtain a perishable crown, but we for an imperishable crown. Therefore I run thus: not with uncertainty. Thus I fight: not as one who beats the air.

(1 Corinthians 9:24-26 NKJV).

Our Guide: Proverbs 29:18

Proverbs, chapter 29, verse 18 in the *Amplified Bible* says, "**Where there is no vision [no redemptive revelation of God], the people perish. . . .**"

We see the interplay of the principle of cause and effect. Where there is no vision, the effect is seen where? It is seen in the people. If you want to test whether or not a vision is present, just look at the people. "Why?" you may ask. Vision is a "redemptive revelation"; this means that vision is not self-focused. Vision is "others-focused." God raises up a man or a woman with a vision to impact the people, so if a vision is present, you will see the effects in the people. This is a universal test for any so-called vision in the Kingdom of God or in society at large. Conversely, if vision is absent, you will see the people perishing.

What Proverbs 29:18 Does Not Say

Proverbs 29:18 says, **"Where there is no vision. . . ."** What it doesn't say is, "Where there is 'no leader. . . .'" This is very significant and not mere semantics.

As mentioned earlier, the continent of Africa is plagued with a lack of vision. Yet the nations on this continent all have leaders in positions of authority. Again, we can see the effects in the people, so we need visionary leaders. A leader without a vision has the potential to become a dictator.

In 2006 we were in an African country holding our seminars. Around that time the economic situation of that country was that of 80 percent unemployment, and according to some of the nationals, approximately one-third of the nation's citizens fled into neighboring countries. Some reported that South Africa was absorbing thousands of people a month from this particular country. The economy was being sustained by those who left the country and were sending back foreign exchange to help their loved ones.

"There is no remedy for undiagnosed problems. You can only fix what you acknowledge."

The currency exchange rate for that country in 2006 was one U.S. dollar to 110,000. In August 2007, it was one U.S. dollar to 210,000. One economist said to us, "We project that in the next six months if the economy continues in this direction, it will collapse."

The leadership of that country failed to take responsibility for their predicament.

So when we talk about leadership without vision, here we see a case study of crisis. There is no remedy for undiagnosed problems. You can only fix what you acknowledge.

Visionary Leaders Needed

Charles De Gaulle once described the qualities of a person who possesses grandeur. "He must aim high, show that he has vision, act on the grand scale, and so establish his authority over the generality of men who splash in the shallow water."[2]

The following is a true story. Four teenage friends prepared to go to their high school prom party. The guys got tuxedos and the ladies got dresses. Each of them paid thirty-dollars to attend the prom. One problem though, neither one of them knew where the prom would take place. So all night long they made stops at different venues that they guessed was the likely place for the prom. Finally, they arrived at the prom with just thirty minutes left to its close. In essence, they paid thirty-dollars each for a thirty-minute prom experience. Why? The level of information they had determined the quality of their journey towards their destination.

Jesus said in Matthew 5:14 NIV **"You are the light of the world. A town built on a hill cannot be hidden."** Whether you are a husband, wife, student, manager, coach, teacher, businessperson, or artist, you need to see yourself as a leader. Leadership is not

"Being called a leader is not necessarily a compliment if you are not a visionary leader. Vision is crucial."

confined to a position or title. If you can influence one person positively then you have the potential to lead. So that means in some way, we are all leaders.

Being called a leader is not necessarily a compliment if you are not a visionary leader. Vision is crucial. It is the way God designed it to be. He says, **"Where there is no vision . . . the people perish . . ."** (AMP). Where there is no redemptive revelation of God, the people perish. Biblical leadership cannot afford to be detached from having a God-given vision.

Leadership without a vision can actually contribute to the acceleration of people perishing. It can speed up the process.

Let's look at Matthew, chapter 15, verse 14 (THE MESSAGE). This is the New Testament counterpart for Proverbs 29, verse 18, where Jesus said, **"When a blind man leads a blind man, they both end up in the ditch."**

> *"For the blind to lead the blind, it means the one being led believes the one leading has sight"*

The fact that they end up in a ditch means there was motion without a clear direction or course of action. So what can we conclude from this? There is a formula for perishing: *The Blind Leading the Way = Ditch or Perishing.*

Again, there is still someone in a position of leadership, but if the people are not infused with sight, they end up perishing anyway or falling into a ditch. This is the consequence. The implication here is this: For the blind to lead the blind, it means that the one being led believes the one who is leading has sight. This is the assumption.

As leaders, when people follow us, they assume that we have some level of sight. That's why they follow us in the first place. But the end result proves to be wrong if we don't have sight.

Ponder this as you examine your own leadership. Are you moving with sight, or are you groping in the dark? The fact is blindness has levels. The idea is to turn our deficits into surpluses, being honest with ourselves when we identify areas in our leadership where we lack insight. We may have sight in one area and have little sight in other areas. When we find out areas where we lack insight, we develop those areas.

"Mindsets are molds and behaviors are patterns. If you do not change the mold, you can't change the pattern."

Someone said, "Any area you are underdeveloped in, make that area a study."

Give this some thought: If your level of excellence in leadership is a five, for instance, you will attract people in the fours and threes who also have a mindset of excellence. Occasionally you may even attract people who are a six or a seven. But over a period of time, when those six and sevens begin to evaluate what you offer in terms of vision, and they don't see you rise up in your level of excellence, they will begin to leave.[3] Mindsets are molds and behaviors are patterns. If you do not change the mold, you can't change the pattern.

So in leadership what you see is critical. When God brings people into your midst, you have to begin to see from God's perspective where these people fit in. Ask yourself, "Where are we taking these people?"

The leader may have lost his or her sight over time along the way. In the introduction we mentioned the lady who said she could now start to enjoy her walk in the Lord. Our book helped her move from "pause" to "play". She could now move on. Often we start out infused with vision, are excited, and thrilled. Then, we encounter obstacles and while we occupy our leadership positions, we may find ourselves going through the motions for years without vision. That is why we have to examine this area constantly.

Precision-guided Missiles

According to Federation of American Scientists, an independent, nonpartisan think tank (Fas.org):

Undoubtedly, one of the most important developments in the history of twentieth century warfare has been the emergence of the precision weapon: the weapon which can be aimed and directed against a single target, relying on external guidance or its own guidance system.

Launched from aircraft, ships, submarines, and land vehicles, or even by individual soldiers on the ground, the precision weapon exemplifies the principle of the low-cost threat that forces a high- cost and complicated defense. Actually, efforts to develop practical precision-guided weapons date to the First World War, though at that time the vision of advocates for such systems far exceeded the actual technological and scientific capability needed to bring them to fruition. But such weapons did appear in the Second World War, in rudimentary though significant form, and it was that experience, and the experience of successor conflicts such as Korea and Vietnam, that gave to us the generation of weapons that now are incorporated in the arsenals of many nations.[4]

Furthermore, Fas.org, revealed the following astounding facts[4]:

In 1944:

108 B-17 bombers (crewed by 1,080 airmen)

dropping 648 bombs had a 96 percent chance of two hits coming close to their intended target.

By contrast during the Gulf War of the early 1990s:

A single strike aircraft (crewed by one or two airmen) dropping two laser-guided bombs had a 100 percent expectation of hitting the target.

In 1944, 108 B-17 bombers crewed by 1,080 airmen [that is, an average of ten men per plane] dropped 648 bombs. The only chance was that two bombs out of 648 would come close to hitting their intended target [no guarantee of actually hitting the target].

In contrast, look at the Gulf War of the early `90s. A single strike aircraft crewed by one or two airmen dropped two laser-guided bombs and had 100 percent expectation of hitting their target.

"A vision never leaves things the way they are. It moves us to change things for the better."

What is the difference between 1944 and the 1990s? What jumps out is, not only can we see the success rate of striking their intended target improve immensely between 1944 and the 1990s, but we also see that they did not have to place as many airmen in harm's way. Can you imagine the casualty rate when you put so many airmen on a mission with little guarantee of success?

Why have things improved from 1944 to the early `90s? First, there was a vision for effectiveness in successfully completing air strikes, and secondly, with fewer casualties. A vision never leaves things the way they are. It moves us to change things for the better.

Perhaps there is a way we are approaching things at present that can be done very differently. If we are not assessing how we do things, time will pass and things will remain the same without much improvement.

Lesson from 1944 and the 1990s

Precision-guided weapons are called "smart bombs," while unguided weapons are called "dumb bombs."

According to Fas.org, Colonel Phillip Meilinger, the commander of the U.S. Air Force School of Advanced Airpower Studies, wrote over sixty years ago: "There is no logical reason why bullets or bombs should be wasted on empty air or dirt. Ideally, every shot fired should find its mark."

In the 1990s, the bombs they used were called precision-guided weapons. They were also called "smart bombs," because they were laser guided. We also have satellite-guided weapons today. In the 1940s they used what were called "unguided weapons," also called "dumb bombs."

So what is the Lesson behind This?

The lesson is simple: don't be a dumb bomb. In relation to God's vision for our lives, we ought not to be unguided weapons. Being an unguided vessel is a great time waster in God's Kingdom agenda. It is time for us to do what God wants us to do with precision and accuracy and accomplish our goals without wasting time or creating casualties. The casualties in this context would be those God has called alongside us to share or follow our vision.

In Summary

Principle 1: If you want to know if a vision is present, you don't look at the leader, you look at the people.

Principle 2: A vision never leaves things the way they are. It moves us to change things for the better.

SECTION II:
DISPELLING
VISION MYTHS

CHAPTER 2
VISION IS NOT PURPOSE

In our ministry teachings, we often use an effective teaching technique we fondly call "compare or contrast." What do we mean by that? Many times to show what a thing is, we have to contrast and show what that thing isn't. We have found that by a process of elimination, when we show what a thing isn't, we can get a better appreciation for what it actually is.

What Vision Isn't

Let's eliminate what vision isn't so we can get a better appreciation for what vision is.

What is the difference between vision and purpose? Purpose points to why a thing exists, while vision sees the outcome of a fulfilled purpose.

> *"Vision sees the potential of purpose."*

Vision sees the potential of purpose. If your vision is limited, you will accomplish very little with your purpose.

For instance, let's examine two people who decide to make their own drinking cups. Person A says he is tired of buying cups. He decides that from now on, all the cups used by his family will be made by him. He will never buy another cup again.

On the other hand, while person B also decides to

manufacture his own drinking cups for his personal use, he says to himself, "I see our city benefiting from the production of our cups . . . I see our State benefiting from the production of our cups . . . and I also see the whole nation benefiting from the production of these cups."

While the purpose of the cups is the same, that is, to drink from, person A sees just enough for his immediate family, however, person B sees an entire nation partaking of his drinking cups. In both scenarios the purpose is the same, but the scope of the vision is different.

Some years ago we had a Bible library on our ministry site that could be downloaded to a person's PC. The digital library numbered over 14,000 pages. It was an in depth library that was a treasure for any bible student or scholar. The problem was that despite the purpose and value of this library, we only had eight downloads in a whole year! I humorously say that the library was gathering digital dust on our site.

One day my brother and I were discussing about the iPhone and he mentioned that someone had told him about app development. The light bulbs came on. I turned to him and said "the Bible library we have can become an app". That is what vision does. It sees the potential of purpose.

When we jumped into the mobile app market, it was so unfamiliar to us. At the time, we modeled after an app developer on the iPhone platform. However, our sights went beyond Apple's iPhone to Android (Google, Kindle, Nook), BlackBerry, Symbian (Nokia), Windows Phone and Tablet (Surface)/PC. As of today we are on all the major mobile platforms with over a quarter of a million downloads. Incidentally, the developer who inspired us on the iPhone platform has not expanded to any other mobile device as of the time of this writing.

The platform you select determines your potential

reach. The bigger the platform, the bigger your reach. As this illustration clearly shows, vision isn't purpose. There could be 2,000, 3,000, 4,000, or 5,000 people functioning in a similar purpose, but having a very different vision.

"The platform you select determines your potential reach. The bigger the platform, the bigger your reach."

Another illustration involves people who have a mission to promote health. One could have a vision to accomplish this purpose through holding health seminars on all health- related subjects. Another could narrow his or her focus to a particular disease like diabetes. Yet another could have a vision for health, but it is a healing ministry, with the laying on of hands to heal. While the purpose may be the same, that is health-related, what each person sees as an outcome may be fundamentally different. That difference is vision.

We can have a purpose, but if we don't have insight into what God is calling us to do, we fall way short of His ultimate plan. Peter and Paul were both called to the same purpose – to preach the gospel – but Peter had a vision to the Jews, and Paul had a vision to the Gentile nations.

In Galatians 2, verse 8 Paul says, **"For God, who was at work in Peter as an apostle to the circumcised, was also at work in me as an apostle to the Gentiles."** As we get a sense of what our purpose is, it is so important that we get a vision for that purpose.

The vision that God gives us is seeing His purpose fulfilled. In other words, it is seeing the scope of how that purpose could impact lives.

God's vision is global in nature. God saw the whole world when He was dealing with Abraham. That's why He changed

> *"Many of us have capped our vision to a certain level, and because of this, we are not rising above that limitation."*

Abram's name to Abraham—from "Exalted Father" to "Father of many nations." He had a vision. God's vision has always been "nations." As you look at the progression, it always comes back to bringing all the nations under one umbrella (the lordship of Jesus Christ).

It is very critical that we stop living beneath our potential. Many of us have capped our vision to a certain level, and because of this, we are not rising above that limitation. Even the people around us are limited to the cap that we have set.

First Corinthians 12:27 AMP says, **"Now you [collectively] are Christ's body and [individually] you are members of it, each part severally and distinct [each with his own place and function]."**

When each of us comes into our function, the world has to watch out. The plan of the enemy is to cause disunity so that we don't grab a hold of God's singleness of purpose. So even though God may give you a specific vision for a region, it will not negate the corporate vision of the Body of Christ. God's vision is always others-focused. He always looks to extend His influence, and He has put us on this planet as ambassadors of His Kingdom.

In Summary

Principle: By understanding what vision isn't, you gain a better appreciation for what vision is. Purpose describes why a thing exists. Vision 'sees' what that purpose can do.

CHAPTER 3
VISION IS NOT A PLAN FOR THE UNEXPECTED

Columbus, after his discovery of America, was persecuted by the envy of the Spanish courtiers for the honors which were heaped upon him by the sovereign; and once at a table, when all decorum was banished in the heat of wine, they murmured loudly at the caresses he received, having, as they said, with mere animal resolution pushed his voyage a few leagues beyond what any one had chanced to have done before. Columbus heard them with great patience, and, taking an egg from the dish, proposed that they should exhibit their ingenuity by making it stand on an end. It went all around; but no one succeeded. "Give it me, gentlemen," said Columbus; who then took it, and, breaking it at one of the ends, it stood at once. They all cried out, "Why! I could have done that." "Yes, if the thought had struck you," replied Columbus; and if the thought had struck you, you might have discovered America."

– Percy[1]

If you drive a car, you are required to possess car insurance. What is car insurance? It is a plan for the unexpected. No one in his or her right mind gets up in the morning, takes his or her car keys, and says, "I want to have an accident today." On the contrary, we have car insurance in the unlikely event that an

27

accident should take place.

Olu recalls an unexpected event in 2006: "We were driving in the Tulsa area on a very uneventful day. From the corner of my eye . . . and in a split second . . . I caught a glimpse of a deer. The deer ran right onto the road. I tried to maneuver the car away, but it was too late. I hit the deer. The front of the car was badly damaged. I didn't get up that day saying, 'Today I'm looking for a deer to hit,' but it happened."

Vision is not like car insurance. Vision is deliberate. Vision does not say, "I am doing this just in case." No, vision goes after something with a very clear objective in mind.

If God had the vision, "I think I may send my Son in case they need Him," we would all be in trouble. But God, in a deliberate act from before the foundation of the world, prepared the Lamb as our Substitute. From the beginning, He had made provision to bring humanity back to Himself.

How deliberate are you about your vision? Is your vision clear? Or is it as "deliberate" as an insurance policy? That's a sobering thought. Deliberateness must be matched with diligence and determination.

The Inventor of Xerography

Chester Carlson worked diligently for years to interest various companies in his invention. Kodak turned it down. Twice the IBM Corporation studied the invention and twice rejected it, once on the advice of the Arthur D. Little Market Analysis Company. The Haloid Corporation, a nearly bankrupt company, finally decided to risk putting money into the invention to see if it could reverse company prospects. It did. Carlson is the inventor of xerography, and the Haloid Corporation is today the Xerox Corporation. IBM, although doing very nicely with computers, has never been able to equal Xerox's dominance of the office copier field.

—M. Hirsh Goldberg[2]

In Summary

Principle: Vision is a deliberate plan unlike an insurance policy which is a plan for the unexpected.

CHAPTER 4

VISION IS NOT CHARISMA

Most people have heard of Bill Gates, cofounder of Microsoft. We all have at one time or another used his computer software. It is obvious that he had a vision for his corporation. If you have seen him interviewed, I don't think that you would say he is charismatic, though he was Microsoft's visionary.

Early on, Bill Gates mentioned his vision of a desktop computer in every home. At the time, no one could really conceive of such a reality. There is nothing charismatic about Bill Gates, but a man of vision he definitely is.

Many people possess charisma, but have no vision. The subtlety about charisma is that it can mask a lack of vision for a while. So while we are drawn to charismatic people and we tend to be excited by charisma, the bottom line is that over time, we see through charisma. Time has a way of being a great revealer. Perception and reality are not always the same. Time will reveal if a person is operating in vision or whether they are simply a man or a woman of charisma.

Universal Test

Having a very magnetic personality doesn't mean a person is a visionary. Again Proverbs 29, verse 18 KJV says, **"Where there is no vision, the people perish. . . ."** This is a universal test for anyone purported to be a person of vision. Over time, if people continue to perish, the person at the helm is not a person of vision though he or she is very charismatic.

In Summary

Principle: Charisma is a magnetic quality; but it is not a substitute for vision.

CHAPTER 5

VISION IS NOT YOUR REPUTATION

A young ensign, after nearly completing his first overseas cruise, was given an opportunity to display his capabilities at getting the ship under way. With a stream of commands, he had the decks buzzing with men, and soon the ship was steaming out the channel en route to the states. His efficiency established a new record for getting a destroyer under way, and he was not surprised when a seaman approached him with a message from the captain. He was a bit surprised, though, to find it a radio message and even more surprised to read: "My personal congratulations upon completing your underway preparation exercise according to the book and with amazing speed. In your haste, however, you have overlooked one of the unwritten rules—make sure the captain is aboard before getting under way."[1]

A reputation is a public persona of a person that is either positive or negative. It is an impression of someone based on something done in the past. A reputation is stuck in the past. It is what people think of us. The danger for men and women of

"Reputation and stagnation are cousins. We should not be focused on how people perceive us based on past accomplishments."

God is that we sometimes ride on our reputation when we have no vision.

What is your present state of focus? What are you pursuing to achieve right now? Reputation and stagnation are cousins. We should not be focused on how people perceive us based on past accomplishments.

In Summary

Principle: Vision is forward thinking, while reputation is an impression based on past achievements.

CHAPTER 6

VISION IS NOT AMBITION

Tower of Babel

The name given to the tower which the primitive fathers of our race built in the land of Shinar after the Deluge (Genesis 11:1- 9). Their object in building this tower was probably that it might be seen as a rallying point in the extensive plain of Shinar, to which they had immigrated from the uplands of Armenia, and so prevent their being scattered abroad. But God interposed and defeated their design by confounding their language, and hence the name Babel, meaning "confusion." In the Babylonian tablets there is an account of this event, and also of the creation and the deluge.[1]

The Stanford Research Institute was making a study of how different people think, how they perceive things differently. They devised a short but succinct test to use in their interviews and proceeded to call in several people from different walks of life. The first to come in was an engineer. The researchers asked him: "Tell us, what does two plus two make?" The engineer didn't hesitate a moment—but simply said, "Well, if you mean in absolute terms—two and two make four." The researchers made their notes, thanked the engineer and dismissed him. Next, they called in an architect. They asked him the same question and he said, "Well, there are several possibilities: two and two make four, but so do three and one—or two and one-half and one and one-half—they also make four. So, it is all a matter of choosing the right option." The researchers thanked him and made their notes. The last of the three to come in was an attorney. They said to him, "What does two and two make?" The attorney looked around furtively, asked if he could close the door for privacy, and then came over close, leaned toward them and said, "Well, tell me, what would you like it to be?"[2]

"Vision is others-focused.... Ambition is self-focused."

We have stressed that vision is not self-focused. Vision is others-focused. Ambition is not vision. In fact, ambition has traits that contradict vision. Ambition is self-focused.

Generally speaking, there is nothing wrong with ambition because we ought to set personal goals for ourselves. However, when it comes to defining Bible-based vision, the test comes down to, "Are people perishing? And if they are perishing, what can be done to stop it?" So vision cannot be self-focused because its goal is to have a positive impact on people. God so loved the world that He gave His only begotten Son. God was focused on reaching out to people.

So how do we test to see if we are "in vision"? Is it self-focused, or is it others-focused?

A true story is told of a very well-known evangelist in America during the height of popularity of tent revivals. The evangelist makes a 3:00 a.m. phone call that wakes up another well-known evangelist. What was the urgent message that couldn't wait? The message was, "I now have a bigger tent than you do." That was his urgent, burning message.

In other words, he was competing with his fellow evangelist. Before then, the other evangelist had a very big tent, but now that his tent could take in more people, he couldn't resist the urge to wake up his "rival" at 3:00 in the morning. The reason: He was self-focused. His was pure ambition. His focus was not God-centered.

Now, what could a bigger tent do? Obviously, a bigger tent meant the capacity to reach more people. That should be the focus. What does the Bible say? Second Corinthians 10, verse 12 says, **"We do not dare to classify or compare ourselves with some who commend themselves. When they measure themselves by themselves and compare themselves with themselves, they are not wise."**

If we have a vision that is God-given, even though we are not necessarily running in the same circles, we are all still a part of the Body of Christ. We have to begin to look at things from that perspective.

What happens when we operate in vision or even ambition? Certain things are done and we accomplish our goals. Are we doing things to really impact the people, or are we doing them just to make a name for ourselves? That is a personal question that we need to answer.

For instance, during World War II, Hitler exhibited ambition on the grandest scale imaginable. He had an ambition that drove him to the point that he slaughtered millions of lives at the altar of his ego. That's an example of a vision in reverse, a demonic vision, impacting several people so severely that even to this day his imprint on history is undeniable. Hitler died decades ago, but his atrocious impact is still being felt today.

The story is told about an old minister who survived the great Johnstown flood. He loved to tell the story over and over in great detail. Everywhere he went he

would spend all his time talking about this great historic event in his life. One day he died and went to heaven and there in a meeting all the saints had gathered together to share their life experiences. The old minister got all excited and ran to Peter (who, naturally, was in charge) and asked if he might tell the exciting story of his survival from the Johnstown flood. Peter hesitated for a moment and then said, "Yes, you may share, but just remember that Noah will be in the audience tonight."[3]

In Summary

Principle: There is a simple test to distinguish a vision from ambition: Vision is always others-focused, but an ambition is self-focused.

CHAPTER 7
VISION IS NOT A FAD

Albert Einstein had a wholesome disregard for the tyranny of custom. Once as a guest of honor at a dinner given for him by the president of Swarthmore College he was called on for a speech. He said, "Ladies and gentlemen, I am very sorry but I have nothing to say and sat down. A few seconds later he stood back up and said, "In case I do have something to say, I'll come back." Six months later he wired the president of the college with the message: "Now I have something to say." Another dinner was held and Einstein made a speech.[1]

Vision is not the reigning thing. I remember in the mid `80s we were still in Nigeria. Young people were coming to the Christian faith in droves. There was a revival.

As we recall, there was a man by the name of Dennis who received Christ into his heart. People were rather amazed. They said, "Wow! Dennis you got born again?" They knew how he was before he got saved, so they asked Dennis, "Dennis, really, are you saved?" Dennis replied, "Yes, I am saved. It's the reigning thing to do."

A vision of God is not determined by trends, polls, or popularity. It is possible sometimes for visionaries to begin to walk in a vision even before their time or perhaps very unfamiliar to their immediate environment. As they walk in their vision, people may say they are crazy.

Many times a visionary at the beginning will be misunderstood because people can't see what he or she sees. But over time, as this person continues to plow away, people will eventually come around and grasp the vision.

Don't be discouraged. If people haven't bought into your vision yet, you are in good company; but you have to keep on plowing and pressing on.

So whether or not it is the reigning thing in the world, God's vision is consistent whether or not people get it.

The vision God has for our lives never changes. He's the One who sees the end from the beginning, so what He sees regarding us never changes. However, the vision will put a demand on us to change to handle what it takes to fulfill it.

In Summary

Principle: Fads and popular trends come and go, but a God-given vision does not fade with time; rather, over time it becomes more relevant.

CHAPTER 8

VISION IS NOT A PROGRAM

Vision should be the determining factor in a program. Putting on a program can facilitate a vision, but it should not be a substitute. It is very possible to have a lot of activities going on with program after program, yet sifting through it all, the entire operation may be void of vision.

Years ago, we received a letter from a pastor that we became acquainted with. For some time we tried to determine what his vision was. In his letter, he listed about thirty things that the church did throughout that year. Yet, after reading everything on the list of programs, we still could not determine the pastor's vision or focus.

Can you imagine what that means to a congregation or an organization? Not being able to clearly articulate why you exist leads to frustration for both the leader and the people he or she is called to serve. The pastor simply had a list of things that he did, but did not have a vision that gave the entire activities context.

"A program without a vision is the equivalent of babysitting adults."

Ask yourself in going from program to program: "Do my programs convey what is central to the vision God has given to me? Can you discern what a program without vision looks like? A program without a vision is the equivalent of babysitting adults. It is keeping you and others busy without a sense of direction. Unfortunately, some misconstrue busyness with productivity. So while a program can be used to facilitate a vision, it is not a substitute for a vision.

In Summary

Principle 1: Programs are no substitute for vision. It is possible to be busy conducting programs but still have little to no concept about what vision is all about.

Principle 2: In an organization, a program without a vision is the equivalent of babysitting adults.

Principle 3: Busyness should not be confused with productivity.

CHAPTER 9

VISION IS NOT A DREAM

Great Dreams

We grow great by dreams. All big men are dreamers. They see things in the soft haze of a spring day, or in the red fire on a long winter's evening. Some of us let these great dreams die, but others nourish and protect them; nourish them through bad days till they bring them to the sunshine and light which comes always to those who sincerely hope that their dreams will come true. Don't let anyone steal your dreams! —Woodrow Wilson.[1]

Think about the following statement: Every visionary is a dreamer, but not every dreamer is a visionary. What does this statement mean? Simply put, a person can have a dream and it only stays in the realm of hope or the realm of wishing.

> *"Every visionary is a dreamer, but not every dreamer is a visionary."*

One trait that is clear about a vision and a visionary is the deliberate hands-on quality to see things happen. Not only do you dream of what you believe will come to pass, you also see yourself in the role you play in bringing that immaterial thought into a concrete, tangible reality.

One working definition of "vision," which we coined almost two decades ago, is this: Vision is an organized system

> *Vision is an organized system of thought, a picture, with a definite course of direction.*

of thought, a picture, with a definite course of direction.

A person who is just a dreamer can be easily detached from an idea, because it's a hands-off state of mind requiring no commitment. The gaps that exist between a dreamer and a visionary are commitment and the value for time. Dreamers use language such as, "Maybe this will happen someday." They don't necessarily see themselves as a force or an agent for change. The reality is that at some point every dreamer has to wake up and face the reality that is before him.

Sometimes people stay for years not taking one step, not even a baby step, towards the vision that God has for them. They always put it off to sometime in the future. But guess what? We own the future in the here and now. We approach the future in the now. If we start taking steps today, in a month's time, we will be further ahead in fulfilling the vision that God has for us. We must depend on God, and we must take steps of faith.

So, even after we dream big dreams, we have to wake up and face reality and take steps towards the fulfillment of that dream. So it is very possible to be a dreamer and not be a visionary. However, it is impossible to be a visionary and not be a dreamer.

After God gives us a vision, He wants us to step up to the plate and start walking it out.

> *"The journey of a thousand miles begins with one step."*

Someone has said, "It's easier to direct a moving car than a car parked on the side of the road." The journey of a thousand miles begins with one step.

Psalm 119, verse 105 KJV says, **"Thy word is a lamp unto my feet, and a light unto my path."**

When we are ready to start a journey, but we don't know how to get to our destination, we will probably pull out a map or use GPS and drive towards the place where we want to go. You can be armed with a map in hand or GPS, but if you don't take steps towards your destination, it will remain a dream unfulfilled.

Martin Luther King Jr. gave an "I Have a Dream" speech. It was a beautiful speech that created vivid pictures in the minds of all who heard it then, and in the minds of those who hear it even now. He saw something ahead, but Martin Luther King Jr. didn't just say, "I have a dream," and stay in his living room! No! Instead, he was a force for positive change.

We are to be both dreamers and visionaries. Sometimes part of what a person sees is beyond that of his or her life's work. While he can start a vision and lay the foundation for it, God can raise up someone else to build upon what has already been conceived. One example is Moses passing the baton to Joshua. The vision was entering into the Promised Land as revealed to Moses but fulfilled by Joshua once Moses was off the scene. That's the way the Kingdom of God works.

In Summary

Principle 1: Every visionary is a dreamer, but not all dreamers are visionaries.

Principle 2: Visionaries see themselves as part of the process. Dreamers can be detached from getting the job done.

CHAPTER 10
LEADERS VERSUS DRIVERS

"When good people run things, everyone is glad, but when the ruler is bad, everyone groans." Proverbs 29:2 The Message (MSG).

One distinct trait regarding vision is this: Vision does not operate in an environment motivated by fear or by the force of the leader. An environment of leadership fostered by fear may be

> *"Vision thrives by inspiration not intimidation."*

indicative of a dictatorship. Vision thrives by inspiration not intimidation. For clarity, let us make a distinction by the use of the term 'drivers' to distinguish a certain leadership style from one that inspires. Please refer to table below:

Drivers are fueled by insecurity	Leaders are fueled by integrity
Drivers assert their position (by intimidation)	Leaders motivate by inspiration
Use force	Use Trust
Motivate by Guilt & Manipulation	Motivate by Vision
Self focused	Others-focused
Seen by the people as a "dictator"	Seen by the people as an "initiator"
Rely on Quotas, see only the 'end result'	Rely on Vision, see the process & end result

Like many teenagers, our first job was working at a popular fast food restaurant located in a very busy shopping center in New York. One particular summer, the restaurant had a sale for a particular burger on the menu. The crowds were huge. There was one major issue; there were only two people working behind the grill: my brother and I!

We were clearly overwhelmed. We made our concerns known to our supervisor, as it was clear that there was no way we could keep up with the demand. In a very detached New York style bluntness, the supervisor blurted out, "I don't care if you die back there, just send me my burgers!" He only cared about the end result, not the process.

In Exodus chapter 5, Moses and Aaron had gone to Pharaoh to command him to "Let My people go, that they may hold a feast to Me in the wilderness." This was the instruction that they had received from God to tell Pharaoh. Instead of giving in, Pharaoh decided to oppress the Israelites.

Verses 4-8 (NKJV) show his response:

"Then the king of Egypt said to them, "Moses and Aaron, why do you take the people from their work? Get back to your labor. And Pharaoh said, "Look, the people of the land are many now, and you make them rest from their labor!" So the same day Pharaoh commanded the taskmasters of the people and their officers, saying, You shall no longer give the people straw to make brick as before. Let them go and gather straw for themselves. And you shall lay on them the quota of bricks which they made before. You shall not reduce it. For they are idle; therefore they cry out, saying, 'Let us go and sacrifice to our God.'"

A driver is only interested in the end result with little to no regard for the process. The 'process' involves people. For the purpose of illustration, say I am having a house built and I have insisted that the house be built in a week. The obvious desired outcome is the finished house, but there would be an enormous strain on the process because of the virtually impossible time constraints. Both the driver and visionary leader create a culture where things are accomplished. The difference is that the visionary leader is both process and outcome conscious.

A visionary leader always thinks about both the outcome and how the vision affects those engaged in the process. Have you ever been in such an environment where you felt coerced? You could not wait till it was over because while you agreed with the goal, you did not enjoy the process. Such fear breeds eye-service and a lack of true loyalty.

The outcome we want to achieve may be noble, but it cannot be achieved by fear, bullying or intimidation.

This is true of a family, a business, a church, or a country. Initiative dies where the value for process is ignored. Remember, process involves consideration for people.

In Summary

Principle 1: Leaders think both about the process and the end result. The 'process' involves people.

Principle 2: Drivers are only concerned about the end result.

Principle 3: Leaders inspire while drivers intimidate.

SECTION III:
WHAT YOU SEE IS WHAT YOU GET

CHAPTER 11
YOUR POINT OF VIEW

Jim Smith went to church on Sunday morning. He heard the organist miss a note during the prelude, and he winced. He saw a teenager talking when everybody was supposed to be bowed in silent prayer. He felt like the usher was watching to see what he put in the offering plate and it made him boil. He caught the preacher making a slip of the tongue five times in the sermon by actual count. As he slipped out through the side door during the closing hymn, he muttered to himself, "Never again, what a bunch of clods and hypocrites!" Ron Jones went to church one Sunday morning. He heard the organist play an arrangement of "A Mighty Fortress" and he thrilled at the majesty of it. He heard a young girl take a moment in the service to speak her simple moving message of the difference her faith makes in her life. He was glad to see that this church was sharing in a special offering for the hungry children...He especially appreciated the sermon that Sunday—it answered a question that had bothered him for a long time. He thought as he walked out the doors of the church, "How can a man come here and not feel the presence of God?" Both men went to the same church, on the same Sunday morning. Each found what he was looking for. What do we look for on Sunday morning?[1]

Ecclesiastes 2:18-23 (NIV) states:

"I hated all the things I had toiled for under the sun, because I must leave them to the one who comes after me. And who knows whether that person will be wise or foolish? Yet they will have control over all the fruit of my toil into which I have poured my effort and skill under the sun. This too is meaningless. So my heart began to despair over all my toilsome labor under the sun. For a person may labor with wisdom, knowledge and skill, and then they must leave all they own to another who has not toiled for it. This too is meaningless and a great misfortune. What do people get for all the toil and anxious striving with which they labor under the sun? All their days their work is grief and pain; even at night their minds do not rest. This too is meaningless."

Notice the consistent repetition of the words "under the sun" and "this too is meaningless." The writer of Ecclesiastes is looking at things purely from a natural point of view. "Under the sun" implies that his way of seeing things did not take God's point of view into account. He was walking by sight, not by faith. This is significant, because he was so conscious of a one-dimensional point of view. God wants us to see things and people from His point of view. When we limit what we do to a natural reward system, ultimately life will feel meaningless.

In Revelation, chapter 4, when God was going to show John the future, He said to him, **"Come up."** In other words, you've seen the past, you are in the present, but for you to see the future, you have to come up to a new dimension. As long as we view life from this limited dimension, life will remain frustrating and meaningless. We are running the first, second, and third legs of this relay race, and at some point, we are going to pass the baton.

What picture does this create for you? I've heard it said, "We are part of something much greater than ourselves." Since a vision is others- focused, it is not about us anyway.

Charisma Magazine highlighted many of God's Generals who have passed on. The big question in this article was, "Who will take their place?" The article stressed the importance of making sure that the transition to the next generation is done accurately to avoid a lack of godly leadership.

Your Point Of View

Some years ago I attended the memorial service of a noted Bible teacher whose ministry and books blessed me greatly when I was growing up. People from all over the United States and overseas came to celebrate his life.

After we have established whatever God has called us to do, we must always think about the next generation. The Charisma article pointed out that many times there is a disconnection between those who have gone ahead and those who are coming behind. So that when they die, it is like, "Okay, what's next?" In fact, this was the motivation behind our

"God's Kingdom is not a Kingdom of superstars. It's a kingdom of servants – royal servants."

book, *The Progenitor Principle: Why You Must Leave a Legacy Behind*. Those who've gone ahead must look back and prepare the next generation. Don't let all that you have die with you. God's Kingdom is not a Kingdom of superstars. It's a kingdom of servants – royal servants.

Unfortunately, many times in the Body of Christ today, men are promoted and treated as superstars. Our adoration and celebration should be to an audience of one – the Lord Jesus. He is to be the driving force in our lives.

In Summary

Principle 1: If you have a negative worldview, you will miss God's intention for placing you on the earth for such a time as this.

Principle 2: Your world view determines the lid you place on your potential.

Principle 3: Those who've gone ahead must look back and prepare the next generation. Don't let all that you have die with you.

CHAPTER 12

ANSWERING SOME QUESTIONS ABOUT VISION

In talking about vision, Proverbs 29, verse 18, is our guide: **"Where there is no vision [no redemptive revelation of God], the people perish . . ."** (AMP). When we mention vision, we are talking about it from God's point of view. This is one of the reasons we make the distinction as to what "vision" is not. Notice, God's heart is always to redeem the world.

A **question** was asked, "Can we say that vision is a catalyst for purpose whereby the flow of it gives value to purpose?" Answer: Absolutely.

A follow-up question: "How do we make sure that the pursuit of our purpose does not overwhelm the vision? Because when the purpose begins to overwhelm the vision, we will not be talking about success and we will not be faithful?"

Answer: Are you familiar with the scripture in Revelation, chapter 3, that describes the church's estimation of itself as rich and fully supplied from its own perspective? But when the Head of the Church, Jesus Christ, comes, what does He say? "You are wretched and naked."

"I know your works, that you are neither cold nor hot. I could wish you were cold or hot. So then, because you are lukewarm, and neither cold nor hot, I will

vomit you out of My mouth. Because you say, 'I am rich, have become wealthy, and have need of nothing' – and do not know that you are wretched, miserable, poor, blind, and naked – I counsel you to buy from Me gold refined in the fire, that you may be rich; and white garments, that you may be clothed, that the shame of your nakedness may not be revealed, and anoint your eyes with eye salve, that you may see. As many as I love, I rebuke and chasten. Therefore be zealous and repent."

– Revelation 3:15-19 NKJV

So we have two different perspectives. One of the main ways many judge success today is by the size of our congregations and the fact that we are on TV. But what is God saying to us?

We have to define "success." We are ministers of God, so we look at success from His point of view. Maybe I have the oversight of only two people, yet God speaks to me, "Well done." Someone else may have a big auditorium and a television ministry. I am not saying that is wrong. But then God says, "You did your own thing. You accomplished many things, but I don't know you." Which of these two ministers is successful in God's eyes?

So we must be careful to not define "success" from the world's point of view. The world's point of view of success is a fat bank account. But from God's estimation, as we saw in the Laodicean church in Revelation, chapter 3, that church had a very grandiose view of itself, yet the Master said, "You are not what you think you are." This is why it is a very sobering thing to maintain a "God view" of our efforts.

In terms of purpose overwhelming vision, it goes back to getting fresh insight from God. I like a prayer that Paul wrote in Colossians, chapter 1, verse 9: **"For this reason, since the day**

we heard about you, we have not stopped praying for you. We continually ask God to fill you with the knowledge of his will through all the wisdom and understanding that the Spirit gives."

A few years ago, this prayer became so real in our ministry. We began to pray: "Lord, we don't want to do our own thing. We want to hear from You."

This is a prayer that you can pray over and over again, and not be outside of faith. Paul says, "Since I heard of your love for the saints, I do not cease to pray for you that you may be filled with the knowledge of His will in all wisdom and spiritual understanding."

As a result of having spiritual understanding, Paul says in Colossians 1:10, **"So that you may live a life worthy of the Lord and please him in every way: bearing fruit in every good work, growing in the knowledge of God."** This is true success according to God's point of view!

So as those called to servant-leadership, we have to cast the vision. We can't just preach a message and ask the people to catch it. An older man of God made this statement: "When you preach a thing over and over and the people are tired of hearing it, they are just beginning to get it."

People live such busy lifestyles, especially in America, that once they leave a church service there are all kinds of things competing for their attention. The Bible tells us to give the more earnest heed to the things which we have heard lest at any time we should let them slip (see Hebrews 2:1 KJV).

Question: "Occasionally, you will find a visionary with a call of God on his life, yet in the denomination to which he belongs, he finds it very difficult to fulfill his vision, because his vision does not fall into the scope of that denomination. This person gets discouraged, because he tries to please his leaders, but he cannot carry out his God-given vision.

"Stepping out of that denomination to pursue the vision God has given him or her may hurt them. In this type of situation, should the person respect the leadership, not willing to be in conflict with them, thus failing to fulfill God's vision? Or should this person ignore the position of leadership and go ahead and do what God has called him or her to do?"

Answer: When we are talking about vision of a church or an individual, I believe that if you are under the umbrella of leadership that is where you will develop your own vision.

This is a very loaded question, because there is not just one answer. If God calls you to join a network, then God knows the vision of that network before you join it. In the event that there is a clash of visions, God will clean it up and do things in a clear way.

If you have a vision that is divorced from the network's vision and you want to go ahead and do it, in the long run, if God is in it, His results will manifest. Jesus said in Luke 7:35 (CJB) "Well, the proof of wisdom is in all the kinds of people it produces." The results that come out of it will show if God is in it.

A lot of the well-known ministers that we know from Tulsa came out of one church. A resident pastor of this church, a young pastor back in the `80s, went to Israel on a mission's trip. He said that God spoke to him about the direction that the church should take. When he came back and shared the vision with the board members and elders of the church, they did not see eye to eye with what he was saying. He didn't start the church, but as I stated, he was a resident pastor.

The board members and elders prayed and they said, "The founding vision for this ministry is not going in the direction that you see God leading you, but we have the peace of

God to release you to do your independent work." This resident pastor's church today is one of the largest churches in Tulsa. When God is in something, you will see results.

That was a multifaceted question. You can look at that question from the angle of a rebel and it would be justified. And you can look at it from the angle of someone who is genuinely called to do something and it would be justified. But the greater question is, "In the end, will God receive the glory out of it?" That is how I would test whether God is in it.

Ecclesiastes 10:10 KJV says, **"If the iron be blunt, and he do not whet the edge, then must he put to more strength: but wisdom is profitable to direct."**

There is something about the Spirit of God infusing wisdom and that does not contradict what we read in Colossians, chapter 1, verse 9, that you be filled with the knowledge of His will. God already anticipates the bumps in the road [the conflicts] before we do, and that's why it is very critical to cooperate with God in the Spirit of unity.

Ephesians, chapter 4, talks about the fivefold ministry gifts. The whole purpose is that we would be unified and that every part of the Body will play some part that makes the whole Body grow. That should be the corporate vision.

SECTION IV:
ACCURATELY DEFINING VISION

CHAPTER 13

WHAT VISION IS

"Every form of foresight begins with insight. Foresight is stifled when insight is shallow." - Kay Taiwo

Proverbs 29, verse 18 AMP says, **"Where there is no vision [no redemptive revelation of God], the people perish...."** In simple terms, vision is the redemptive revelation of God. Vision sees the end from the beginning. It captures the heart of God, and then translates it into practical steps that lead to restoration, salvation, community, and empowerment.

In Genesis, chapter 1, God created the earth; then He placed man in it. Genesis 1:26 in the NKJV states: **"Then God said, 'Let Us make man in Our image, according to Our likeness; let them have dominion. . . .'"** This verse is pregnant with divine purpose. Vision always seeks to restore, build, save, encourage, free, empower, uphold, and redeem others. The nature of a God-given vision is seen in its love for others.

"Vision always seeks to restore, build, save, encourage, free, empower, uphold, and redeem others."

There are three principles that arise from this verse:

1.   The Principle of Origin;

2.   The Principle of Identity; and

3.   The Principle of Destiny.

The Principle of Origin

Genesis 1:26 says **"Then God said...."** If the Bible did not identify the person speaking, it would leave room for guessing and doubt. But it tells us, **"God said."** If the Bible said, "So-and-so's Great Grandfather said," we could pull the statement apart and say, "So-and-so's Great Grandfather could be wrong." But, the Bible eliminates any doubt or question as to who was speaking. The Bible says, **"God said,"** so man was not man's idea; man was God's idea.

"In a remote Swiss village stood a beautiful church. It was so beautiful, in fact, that it was known as the Mountain Valley Cathedral. The church was not only beautiful to look at--with its high pillars and magnificent stained glass windows--but it had the most beautiful pipe organ in the whole region. People would come from miles away--from far off lands-- to hear the lovely tones of this organ.

"But there was a problem. The columns were still there--the windows still dazzled with the sunlight--but there was an eerie silence. The mountain valley no longer echoed the glorious fine tuned music of the pipe organ.

"Something had gone wrong with the pipe organ. Musicians and experts from around the world had tried to repair it. Every time a new person would try to fix it the villagers were subjected to sounds of disharmony, awful penetrating noises which polluted the air.

"One day an old man appeared at the church

door. He spoke with the sexton and after a time the sexton reluctantly agreed to let the old man try his hand at repairing the organ. For two days the old man worked in almost total silence. The sexton was, in fact, getting a bit nervous. Then on the third day--at high noon--the mountain valley once again was filled with glorious music. Farmers dropped their plows, merchants closed their stores--everyone stopped what they were doing and headed for the church. Even the bushes and trees of the mountain tops seemed to respond as the glorious music echoed from ridge to ridge.

"After the old man finished his playing, a brave soul asked him how he could have fixed the organ, how could he restore this magnificent instrument when even the world's experts could not. The old man merely said it was an inside job. "It was I who built this organ fifty years ago. I created it--and now I have restored it."

"That is what God is like. It is He who created the universe, and it is He who can, and will, and is in the process of restoring it."[1]

The Principle of Identity

God didn't just say that He was going to make a creature. This creature had an identity. God said, **"Let us make man in Our image...."** This speaks of man's identity. Man was to be God's image bearer on the earth. The word "image" is the Hebrew word tselem meaning a representative figure. When you saw the man, you saw his God. He was an ambassador of Heaven on earth.

For many years I questioned God as I was reading Genesis, chapter 2, verse 19. It says that God brought all of the animals to Adam to see what he would name them.

I asked God, "Why did You have this man name all of the animals?" God could have named the animals Himself. You have to understand that chapter 2 comes before the fall of man in chapter 3. Chapter 2 is a picture of the exercise of dominion. Man was made in God's image, and he was exercising dominion as God's representative.

Notice, when Adam named an animal, God didn't come back and say, "Wait a minute, Adam. You missed it. What you called a lion should have been named a dog." God didn't do that. At this time, sin wasn't in the picture. Man was in complete synchrony with his God so that when he spoke, God said, "Yes, that's the name." God approved what Adam declared.

But the interesting thing is this. Even though man sinned in Genesis, chapter 3, Adam bore humanity in him; and from Adam, the seed of sin has been passed through all generations. Though man has sinned and is in a fallen state, the ability to name was never recalled. Even in our day, men are still calling. We create things, and even though men sometimes don't understand God, they are still using the ability to call.

Forty years ago no one in the populace knew what the Internet was. Today it's a common word. Man created it and then he named it. Sometimes in his pride, he thinks that the ability to call came from him. But no, it came from God.

The Principle of Destiny

The third principle is the principle of destiny. Within verse 26 of Genesis, chapter 1, God says, **"...let them** [man] **have dominion..."** (NKJV). This speaks of man's destiny. Man came from God, and he was God's image bearer. Man was to exercise dominion over creation, but in Genesis, chapter 3, something happens. Man began to listen to another voice.

There are four voices that testify about us on this planet:

- The voice of God;

- The voice of Satan;

- The voice of man or the world around us; and

- The voice of self.

I have found out that the voice you and I embrace is the voice that eventually becomes our own. We have to identify, "What voice am I embracing? Am I embracing the voice of God for my destiny?"

In Genesis, chapter 3, man falls, but the interesting thing is this: man's fall didn't take God by surprise, because in God the answer exists before the problem appears.

> *"...man's fall didn't take God by surprise, because in God the answer exists before the problem appears."*

God is a God of vision and a God of foresight. That's the redemptive revelation of God. He saw men gathered again in Himself, through His Son, and that is the power of vision. When God gives you a vision, He anticipates that this vision is an answer to a problem that may not exist yet in the eyes of man. This is what we mean by the redemptive revelation of God.

God is in the business of preserving and restoring. Joseph had a dream at seventeen years of age. At this time in his life, he did what a person in the prime of their youth would do. They get excited, but they don't necessarily understand the full context of what they see and what they would have to become for the fulfillment of that dream.

In connection to Joseph, as mentioned earlier,

"Visionaries are dreamers, but not all dreamers are visionaries." Regarding Joseph, God was in the picture from the beginning until the time of the fulfillment of his dream – that Joseph would be elevated and he would be a preserver. Some scholars have said that Joseph was a type of Jesus and foreshadowed what Jesus would do.

In Summary

Principle: Proverbs 29, verse 18, is our guide: "Where there is no vision [no redemptive revelation of God], the people perish..." (AMP). Vision is a redemptive revelation of God to impact and empower people for the kingdom of God.

CHAPTER 14

VISION SEES THE OUTCOME

The Telephone

Alexander Graham Bell, the inventor of the telephone, an invention without which the business world of today could not even begin to function, was hard pressed to find a major backer. In 1876, the year he patented the telephone, Bell approached Western Union, then the largest communications company in America, and offered it exclusive rights to the invention for $100,000. William Orton, Western Union's president, turned down the offer, posing one of the most shortsighted questions in business history: "What use could this company make of an electrical toy?" There is, however, some poetic justice in the corporate world. The telephone eventually consumed the lion's share of the market that Western Union had dominated. —M. Hirsh Goldberg.[1]

The Alliance for Nonprofit Management says:

"A vision is a guiding image of success formed in terms of a contribution to society...It is a description in words that conjures up a similar picture for each member of the group of the destination of the group's work together."

"A vision is a guiding image of success formed in terms of a contribution to society." So a vision is not self-focused. It is a guiding picture that is formed in terms of contributions to society.

In other words, when someone reads our vision statement, it should bring up certain things in their minds about how it is going to impact our world.

"It is a description in words that conjures up a similar picture for each member of a group of the destination of the group's work together." When people come to this organization and they hear the vision statement, they should have a clear and compelling picture of what the organization is about and what impact the organization is called to make.

If I meet one person on the street here and move to another city and meet another person who is a part of the same network, I should get a non-conflicting picture about your organization.

Vision sees the outcome. For example, God saw the salvation of man before the foundation of the earth and made provision for it. He sees the outcome in eternity. Then, in time He starts the process. We have to pattern things after our Maker, God.

> *"Vision sees the outcome means God sees the end from the beginning."*

Vision sees the outcome means God sees the end from the beginning. He may give you a vision that initially may not make sense to you or to the people around you.

This is what happened with Joseph. He didn't understand what God had revealed to him in its full context. Then when he shared it in a presumptuous manner, the people around him didn't appreciate or understand it either. Many times this is what causes conflict.

When we don't understand someone's vision, it creates room for conflict. This is why there needs to be a clarification of the vision. Constantly casting the vision before the people is very critical.

"Constantly put the vision before the people"

If it's a building project, constantly cast the vision so that the people catch it. There is something about human nature. Just because we shared our vision once does not mean that the people got it. Constantly put the vision before the people. Rehearse it, make it clearer, and find creative ways to establish or communicate the same vision over and over again.

Vision sees the end from the beginning, and then with God's help, creates a path towards what it has seen and brings the people along. For people to be brought along, they must catch the vision. This brings synergy to the project.

In Summary

Principle 1: Vision sees the 'outcome' it wants and takes definite and deliberate steps to reach its goal.

Principle 2: Vision sees possibilities beyond the familiar.

Principle 3: Constantly put the vision before the people. Rehearse it, make it clearer, and find creative ways to establish or communicate the same vision over and over again.

CHAPTER 15

EXPANDING YOUR HORIZONS

The year was 1987, the place was Nigeria. The word of God was spreading rapidly across the south as young people in the hundreds, and even thousands embraced Jesus Christ as Lord and Savior. Parents generally became concerned and nervous as they saw their children dissatisfied with the traditional institution of denominationalism. Such was the surge of young people coming to Christ that Islam was threatened.

This threat seemed to escalate in the northern part of Nigeria as a result of an invasion of the Gospel message of Jesus Christ. This invasion sent a jolt of shock waves across the Muslim community. This set off an unfortunate course of events leading to a violent protest, which resulted in the killing of several Christians, and the burning down of over one hundred church buildings.

For fear that this violence would spread into the schools, the government of Nigeria decided to place a ban on every religious association on the school premises across the country. Our school Christian fellowship President casually explained that the fellowship would stop and resume in a year's time (that is, 1988).

My brother, a few friends and I expressed our concerns about the negative impact this would have on the new converts from Islam. For many of them, the Christian fellowship was the only source for receiving teaching from the word of God. The Christian fellowship President however, maintained his casual stand. About six of us concerned brothers in Christ decided to meet weekly to keep ourselves stirred up spiritually. Before long we were meeting at an Assemblies of God Church on the outskirts of our school. We grew to ninety people. So was the reward of our diligence that despite the ban, we grew in numbers behind the scenes. Our growth now exceeded the numbers we had before the ban was in place. The year 1988 came around and the ban was lifted; our fellowship venue resumed on the school grounds with a regular weekly attendance averaging 125 to 150 students.

"Every form of foresight begins with insight. Foresight is stifled when insight is shallow."

The lesson from this experience taught me the importance of foresight. Foresight is what separates the achievers from the underachievers. Every form of foresight begins with insight. Foresight is stifled when insight is shallow.

"Before I formed thee in the belly I knew thee; and before thou camest forth out of the womb I sanctified thee, and I ordained thee a prophet unto the nations. Then said I, Ah, Lord GOD! behold I cannot speak: for I am a child. But the Lord said unto me, Say not I am a child: for thou shalt go to all that I shall send thee, and whatsoever I command thee thou shalt speak."

(Jeremiah 1 verses 5-7)

Many people who are mediocre in a given area have perhaps little knowledge of their untapped potential, or perhaps they are exercising effort in an area that God has not ordained for them. When you find your niche, firmly embracing the will of God that shows up strong in what you DO THE BEST most of the time, you are now ready to maximize your potential rather than just maintain it. (Read Proverbs 24 verses 3-5).

Jeremiah's meeting with God gave him some personal insight. This insight produced foresight regarding his future ministry. By introducing Jeremiah to his true identity and purpose, God successfully expanded his horizon. The Merriam-Webster dictionary defines 'horizon' as:

(1) The line marking the apparent junction of earth and sky;
(2) Range of outlook or experience.

So the Lord broadens his outlook. God's range of outlook differs from our perspective. Perspective means the view of things (as object or events) in their true relationships or relative importance (MW dictionary). While Jeremiah's view was limited to his constrained societal conditioning and way of thinking, God's view was from a divine, eternal perspective. God will use the vision for your future to blot out the nightmare of your past average existence. Jeremiah was timid to speak the word of God and face the people. These inbuilt constraints were revealed to him by God (see Jeremiah 1 vs.7-8).

It is imperative, as we have seen that we learn to live our lives by seeing it from God's point of view. Life demands that we make choices that will positively affect our lives. The quality of the choices we make reflect the maturity and quality of our perspective or outlook on life. Therefore, true maturity is a measure of how much life is lived from the perspective of God. The more of God's perspective we have on a subject, be it marriage, business, raising children, counseling, and making major decisions, the greater is the potential of us realizing His ultimate best.

"Two men looked out from prison bars. One saw mud, one saw stars." In the pursuit of the fullness of human life, everything depends on this frame of reference, this habitual outlook, this basic vision which I have of myself, others, life, the world, and God. What we see is what we get."[1]

Two Powerful Concepts

From Jeremiah 1 verses 5-7 emerge two powerful provocative concepts. These concepts apply to any area of life's issues we face. These two concepts are very much interwoven with one's vision for life. Vision can be defined as *an organized system of thought, a picture, with a definite course of direction.* This can apply to any area of our lives. Now back to our two concepts!

These two concepts are:

(1)   The big picture; (Jeremiah 1 verse 5).

(2)   The details; (Jeremiah 1 verses 7-19).

Many pursue their vision for life from their perception of the big picture and of what they want accomplished. This is where the problem lies. You see, the strategy to fulfilling any vision does not emerge from the big picture. The reason is that the big picture is a generalization of what you want accomplished - an overall agenda.

For instance, in boardrooms across America, corporate teams bring ideas and concepts with the aim that their peers and superiors will buy into them. Once an idea is adopted, they then develop a detailed analysis of how each part fits to make that concept a reality. The 'big picture' is the idea; while the 'details' followed help bring it to pass. You see, the strategy to fulfilling any vision is predicated upon following specific details. In fact, the strategy to fulfilling any vision is synonymous with the details.

The 'details' convey how to reach your goal. For example, if your big picture is attending a college of your choice, the strategy to successfully get this goal accomplished would be to take the entrance examination then you would apply to the school of your choice by filling the required forms etc. Notice that the mere 'conception' of going to college does not come into fruition until you understand and implement a strategy. By working through the details that stand as the main challenge to you seeing your goal accomplished, you increase your chances for admission to the college of your choice.

So we see that the strategy is not in the big picture, but in the details. You only become fulfilled to the degree that you successfully follow the instructions. The wall of Jericho did not fall because of the big picture God conveyed to Israel; it fell because Joshua and the Israelites followed the strategy God outlined regarding the big picture (which in this case was the falling of the city walls). If Joshua ran with the big picture without following the strategy God gave, which meant they had to march around the walls of Jericho, they would have never seen their big picture turn into a reality! Another example is Noah. Genesis 6 verses 12-13 as taken from the Amplified Bible read:

"And God looked upon the world and saw how degenerate, debased, and vicious it was, for all humanity had corrupted their way upon the earth and lost their true direction. "God said to Noah, I INTEND TO MAKE AN END TO ALL FLESH, for through men the land is filled with violence; and behold, I WILL DESTROY THEM AND THE LAND."

Notice that the words in capital letters convey the big picture of the judgment of God which was about to fall on the people of Noah's day. Up until this time, nothing is said about how God was going to get this accomplished. All we know is that judgment was coming. To assume how God was going to do it would be dangerous. If God just left Noah with only this information, he would have been left in the dark big time. Thank

God, He did not! In Genesis 6 verses 14-15 (AMP) it reads thus:

> **"MAKE YOURSELF an ark of gopher or cypress wood; make in it rooms (stalls, pens, coops, nests, cages, and compartments) and cover it inside and out with pitch (bitumen). And this is THE WAY YOU ARE TO MAKE IT: the length of the ark shall be 300 cubits, its breadth 50 cubits, and its height 30 cubits [that is, 450 ft. x 75 ft. x 45 ft.]."**

Need we say more? I encourage you to read the rest of this chapter, and the two following. You can see that some details of God's strategy are beginning to emerge. God gives very precise details as to how things are to be done. The big picture as you can see does not require physical labor, but the strategy does. The strategy is where the rubber meets the road. The exercise of faith is the deciding factor; for without it, no great idea can be conceived or accomplished.

> *"The strategy is where the rubber meets the road."*

These concepts once understood and fully embraced will revolutionize our effectiveness in any given area of life we undertake.

Food for Thought

There are three aspects that affect the realization of your God-given vision before its implementation. They are as follow:

(1) Outcome (clear goal).

(2) Methods (tools).

(3) Resources (provision for your vision).[2]

These three must be prioritized in the order given above. The reason is that before you talk about your tools or methodology and resources, which many times are self-limiting at the beginning, you ought to have a clear directive of the goal you are out to accomplish. Once this goal or desired outcome is in place, it becomes easier to outline your method, and will consequently help you make an estimate of the amount of resources required. If you focus on your resources first, you may be discouraged from dreaming big especially if you have limited resources.

Sound Identity

+ Biblical Meditation

+ Corresponding Actions

= Success

"This Book of the Law shall not depart out of your mouth, but you shall meditate on it day and night, that you may observe and do according to all that is written in it. For then you shall make your way prosperous, and then you shall deal wisely and have good success."

—Joshua 1 vs. 8, (THE AMPLIFIED BIBLE).

This passage is so profound, yet extremely simple in its ability to offer practical tips for biblical success. The reason we meditate is for the purpose of 'observing to do.' Success is achieved in any given area to the degree that you give consistent thought to the word of God on that subject. We are admonished in this passage to meditate so that the truth we have already embraced becomes more productive in our lives. As we become more aware of the reality of God's will for our individual lives, we are in a position to "observe to do" what His will declares. This is what brings good success. The word of God cannot be observed if it is not known.

"Where there is no vision the people perish: but

he that keepeth the law, happy is he." (Proverbs 29 vs. 18, KJV). Those who keep the law (or word of God) are the happy ones because of what it produces for them. Success does not just happen. You must put a biblical spotlight on every area you desire to succeed in.

Please note: the journey of life involves a balancing act between the big picture and the strategy. Many people get so caught up with the details that they forget what they set out to accomplish in the first place. Likewise never get so caught up with the big picture that you do not consider the process. Additionally, it's not good to be so wrapped up in the process that you forget the essence of life and relationships. Balance must be seriously considered.

Albert Einstein was considered an uneducable slow learner in school. This very man wrote the 'Theory of Relativity' at age twenty-six. Today, he goes down in history as one of the brightest minds of the twentieth century. Arguably, he is the most famous scientist of the modern era. The truth is that no failure or human verdict is credible enough to stifle success if we embrace what God says about us.

> *"The truth is that no failure or human verdict is credible enough to stifle success if we embrace what God says about us."*

We meditate to succeed in pleasing God. Meditation heightens our awareness of God's plan for our lives by producing in us a conscious knowledge. It is this conscious knowledge of the purposes, plans, and pursuits of God's will that produces a tangible reality. If there is nothing else you remember on the subject of meditation, remember this, we meditate in order to "observe to do" the word of God. When this is in place it will ensure that we produce (in practical ways), the will of God in our lives on this planet.

"Never tell anyone it can't be done. God may have been waiting for centuries for somebody ignorant enough of the impossible to do that very thing."[3]

In Summary

Principle 1: Every form of foresight begins with insight. Foresight is stifled when insight is shallow.

Principle 2: The more God-given insight you receive, the greater will be your horizons.

THE VISION GUIDED LIFE

CHAPTER 16
THE BIG PICTURE AND THE DETAILS

Paint a Broad Picture

As you give others an opportunity to share your dream, paint a broad picture for them so that they can catch your vision. You may want to include the following: A Horizon: to help them see the incredible possibilities ahead. The Sun: to give them warmth and hope. Mountains: to represent the challenges ahead. Birds: to inspire them to soar like eagles. Flowers: to remind them to stop and smell the roses, to enjoy the journey along the way. A Path: to offer direction and security, to give assurance that you will be leading them the right way. Yourself: to demonstrate your commitment to the dream and to them. Them: to show where they fit in and to communicate your belief in them. —John Maxwell.[1]

The big picture could be likened to comprehension, and the details or strategy can be likened to the competency part. This information is key, for it is possible to grab a hold of the big picture, yet have no idea about God's strategy.

As stated earlier, Joshua and the Israelites were told that they were going to conquer Jericho. This statement alone put a picture in their minds. The day this was revealed to them, Jericho was about to be defeated. The natural inclination would be to take up your sword, spear, your bows and arrows, and go out and fight, but that wasn't God's strategy in this case.

While the big picture was the defeat of Jericho, God had a specific strategy in mind. If Joshua and the Israelites had not followed God's strategy, they would have been defeated.

"So the victory or defeat of a vision depends on whether or not the right strategy is employed."

While we may have a glimpse of the big picture in a situation, we also need God's strategy. In fact, it is in the strategy that the rubber actually meets the road. That is where the work is involved, because you can receive a big picture in a moment of time, but it takes a process to fulfill the vision, which is in the strategy. So the victory or defeat of a vision depends on whether or not the right strategy is employed.

As an illustration, we will assume that someone is having problems with ants in their home. The man of the house mentions this to a friend. The friend says, "Here is the strategy that I employed. My house had ants, so I got a blow torch and used the flames to get rid of the ants."

The guy with the current ant invasion said, "Okay, I am going to do the same thing." He got a blow torch and he got rid of the ants, but in the process, his house caught on fire and burned down because he employed a strategy without taking proper precautions. Result: He got rid of the ants and his house too!

You have to be careful about the strategy you employ. While you have an outcome in mind, are you employing the right strategy? Is that the most effective strategy to employ?

Another case in point in scripture is Noah. Sometimes things don't make sense when God reveals His method or plan.

During this period of biblical history, no one had ever heard about a flood or rain. Suddenly God introduces a big picture: "I am going to destroy the inhabitants of the earth because of their consistent wickedness and constant rebellion to My purposes. I am going to eliminate them, and there is going to be a flood. I want you to build an ark, Noah."

The Bible says that it took a hundred and twenty years for Noah to build the ark before the rains came pouring down. Can you imagine Noah going to his neighbors, and saying, "You better get ready. Rain is coming." They probably would have thought he was crazy. If God had said, "Rain is coming, and I'm going to destroy the earth," and He didn't give any more details beyond that, He would have left Noah in confusion.

God could have had a plan and said, "I want you to meet Me under the tree. Gather your family, because there is going to be rain, but I will suspend you in the air. There will be a canopy around you. That is how I am going to preserve you from the flood."

But no, God used a strategy that was very unique to Noah. God told him to build an ark. I am sure as he was building, his neighbors came around and said, "Something is wrong with this guy!" They must have thought that something was going on, because Noah just kept on building the ark.

God had a big picture of both the destruction of the wicked and the preservation of a remnant. He had a specific strategy.

In Genesis, chapter 6, verses 15-16, God gave Noah specific details and dimensions.

"This is how you are to build it: The ark is to be three hundred cubits long, fifty cubits wide and thirty cubits high. Make a roof for it, leaving below the roof an opening one cubit high all around. Put a door in

the side of the ark and make lower, middle and upper decks."

God was so specific with His strategy, because He knew exactly what He was doing. That is why, just like Noah, if we are getting instructions from God and receiving a God-given strategy with precision, the results will show it.

In Summary

Principle: The big picture is different from a strategy; having a vision does not mean you understand what strategy you ought to use. This is where we must apply the principle in Matthew 7:7-8: "Ask, and it will be given to you; seek, and you will find; knock, and it will be opened to you. For everyone who asks receives, and the one who seeks finds, and to the one who knocks it will be opened."

CHAPTER 17
JOSEPH FINALLY UNDERSTOOD HIS "VISIONS"

God gave Joseph a dream. Time is a revealer. If God is in something, over time we will see it. If the dream was Joseph's own idea, then it would have failed. Look at all of the obstacles that Joseph went through. If God was not in the picture, eventually things would not have turned out the way they did.

> *"Time is a revealer."*

In Genesis 39, the scripture says, **"And God was with Joseph."** When things were good, God was with Joseph; and when things were not good, God was with Joseph. In the latter part of Joseph's life, we see that God indeed was with Joseph.

In Genesis, chapter 45, Joseph is about to reveal himself to his brothers who have been coming down to Egypt [where Joseph is second in command to Pharaoh] to get food. Joseph was having a dialogue with his brothers who didn't recognize him. Finally, Joseph makes himself known to them. Now the understanding on Joseph's part as to why God sent him ahead is revealed.

Verses 1-7 of Genesis, chapter 45 (NIV), say:

"Then Joseph could no longer control himself before

all his attendants, and he cried out, "Have everyone leave my presence!" So there was no one with Joseph when he made himself known to his brothers. And he wept so loudly that the Egyptians heard him, and Pharaoh's household heard about it. Joseph said to his brothers, "I am Joseph! Is my father still living?" But his brothers were not able to answer him, because they were terrified at his presence. Then Joseph said to his brothers, "Come close to me." When they had done so, he said, "I am your brother Joseph, the one you sold into Egypt! And now, do not be distressed and do not be angry with yourselves for selling me here, because it was to save lives that God sent me ahead of you. For two years now there has been famine in the land, and for the next five years there will be no plowing and reaping. But God sent me ahead of you to preserve for you a remnant on earth and to save your lives by a great deliverance."

> *"Here we see that the answer existed before the problem manifested."*

Here we see that the answer existed before the problem manifested. When Joseph, at seventeen, was getting the vision of what his life would be, he didn't understand the context. So in his lack of understanding, he said (paraphrased), "I saw my sheaf of grain standing up and your sheaves of grain bowing down to me." He didn't know the context of what that meant, but now he essentially said to them, "Do not be distressed about selling me into slavery, because it was God who sent me ahead of you to preserve for you a remnant."

Vision is never about you. A God-given vision is always about others. Joseph's vision wasn't about him. Although as a teenager, Joseph might have been self-focused, when God matured Joseph, he got to a point where he could receive and accept the responsibility of preserving others.

As Joseph revealed himself to his brothers, he said, "I understand that God sent me ahead of you to preserve for you a remnant."

God always makes provision for the future. We may not initially understand a vision, because vision usually starts as a seed. It has been said, *"Everything begins in seed form and grows into an experience."*

When God starts a thing, He drops a seed in us. That seed has to grow. In the case of Moses, he saw an Egyptian fighting a Hebrew and he intervened. Something inside of him said, "This thing ought not to be." Moses went out to see his brethren and check on their well-being. God had planted that seed in him about His people and His rule with His people, even though Moses didn't have a full understanding of it until forty years later. But in his immature understanding that things ought not to be this way, Moses reacted rashly.

"When God starts a thing, He drops a seed in us. That seed has to grow."

That wasn't God's way, even though the seed had been planted in Moses. Moses then goes through the wilderness experience where God began to strip certain things away and then affirm and confirm certain things within him. Then it became clear to him how he was to handle the responsibility.

It was the same way with Joseph. He could now handle the responsibility of the vision that God had given him much earlier at age seventeen.

God wants to deliver, preserve, and uplift people. He

wants to take them to a new level in His will and purpose.

In Summary

Principle 1: Wisdom and maturity are requirements for effectively executing a vision.

Principle 2: When God starts a thing, He drops a seed in us. That seed has to grow.

CHAPTER 18

GOD'S VISION REVEALED

John 3:16 NKJV says, **"For God so loved the world that He gave His only begotten Son, that whoever believes in Him should not perish but have everlasting life."**

Proverbs 29:18 AMP says, **"Where there is no vision [no redemptive revelation of God] the people perish...."**

Three words jump out in each of these verses: **"should not perish"** and **"the people perish."** So vision is tied to the redemptive revelation of God. And so is the love of God.

From the two verses above it becomes clear: vision and love share the same interest. They are both others- focused.

> *"...vision and love share the same interest. They are both others-focused."*

The Son of God, Jesus Christ, took on human form. He didn't come for Himself, because He could have stayed in heaven. Philippians, chapter 2 verse 7 [NIV], says **"...he made himself nothing."** Jesus took on the form of a human being and went through the human experience for us. This is one of the reasons why, during His temptations in the wilderness in Matthew, chapter 4, Satan's objective was aimed at getting Jesus to focus on Himself, which would have resulted in Him taking his eyes off of His mission.

This is where we go back to motive. Jesus' answer is an answer that we should all live by: **"Man shall not live on bread alone, but on every word that comes from the mouth of God."** (Matthew 4:4, NIV).

The words out of the mouth of God are the counsel of God, and His words are infused with vision. When we embrace the one voice we spoke of earlier, God's voice, it will take us to a new level. We will see life from God's point of view, that is, the redemptive revelation of God to redeem mankind and bring us back to Himself.

In Summary

Principle 1: God's heart is demonstrated in this verse: "For God so loved the world that He gave His only begotten Son, that whoever believes in Him should not perish but have everlasting life." John 3:16 NKJV.

Principle 2: God wants us to embrace Him as the Source of our life.

CHAPTER 19

HOW A VISION IS OBTAINED

"...It is written, 'Man shall not live by bread alone, but by every word that proceeds from the mouth of God.'" (Matthew 4:4 NKJV).

God's Word is the foundation for discovering His plans and purposes.

God will use each person in a different way, taking each individual on a different path to see His plans and purposes come to pass. This is why we have to be in tune with God to get clear direction.

Earlier I shared about Colossians, chapter 1, verse 9. It is interesting that scholars have called Ephesians 1:17 a twin scripture to this verse in Colossians.

Let's look at Ephesians, chapter 1, verse 17, which is a powerful prayer by the Apostle Paul to a different part of the Body of Christ. While Colossians 1:9 was to the church at Colossae, this verse in Ephesians is to the church at Ephesus:

Let's look at Ephesians 1:15-20 (NIV):

"For this reason, ever since I heard about your faith in the Lord Jesus and your love for all God's people, I have not stopped giving thanks for you, remembering you in my prayers. I keep asking

that the God of our Lord Jesus Christ, the glorious
Father, may give you the Spirit of wisdom and
revelation, so that you may know him better. I pray
that the eyes of your heart may be enlightened.
[New Living Translation (NLT) says, "I pray that your
hearts will be flooded with light..."] in order that you
may know the hope to which he has called you, the
riches of his glorious inheritance in his holy people,
and his incomparably great power for us who believe.
That power is the same as the mighty strength He
exerted when he raised Christ from the dead and
seated him at his right hand in the heavenly realms."

Paul prayed without ceasing – not a one-time effort. From
the very beginning, Paul said, "I don't cease to pray for you
that the God of our Lord Jesus Christ, the Father of glory, may
give you a Spirit of wisdom and revelation in the knowledge of
Him." In other words, Paul, as in his own example in Philippians,
chapter 3, makes the statement, **"That I may know him."**
According to scholars, the Apostle Paul was thirty years in the
ministry when he wrote the book
of Philippians. He didn't say, "I
know Him." He said, **"That I
may know him,"** which means
you never arrive at a static point
in God.

*"...you never arrive at a
static point in God."*

There are depths in God. The deeper you go in God, the
deeper you need to go in God. Paul, a thirty-year veteran in the
ministry, says, **"That I may know him."** This means it is not
just a casual knowing and it's not a casual knowledge. This is
what we see in Ephesians, chapter 1. The more we know Him,
the more we know His mind.

In Psalm 103:7 we learn that **"He made known his ways
unto Moses, his acts unto the children of Israel."** Moses knew
the motivating factors for God's acts, but the Israelites just saw

the acts of God. They did not know the heart of God.

When we begin to know God, His heart and His vision are exposed. So to understand a vision, we must know God's heart and see from His point of view.

Webster's Dictionary defines the word "vision" as unusual discernment or foresight; the act or power of seeing.

When God gives us a vision, we may grasp it and comprehend it, but that doesn't mean that we are capable of accomplishing it. One of the things about walking with God is that revelation is progressive.

Comprehension is Not Competency

Comprehension and competency are not synonymous. What do I mean by that? Jesus made a very powerful statement. He said, **"...Follow me, and I will make you fishers of men"** (Matthew 4:19 KJV). What does this statement imply? **"Follow me."** The disciples didn't really know what it would take to become the kind of people who, when Jesus left in three years after fulfilling His ministry, could take over and continue His work. But in the process of following Him, they became competent.

For the disciples to leave their nets and follow Jesus, they must have had a certain level of comprehension as to what Jesus' vision was about and where His mission might take them. But that doesn't mean they were competent.

Jesus didn't say, "Follow Me. Go do the work." Rather, implicitly He said, "Follow Me and in the process I will make you..." So it is in following Jesus that we become

"The first step is to follow Him. His responsibility to make us comes after our obedience to follow."

competent kingdom agents. The first step is to follow Him. His responsibility to make us comes after our obedience to follow. It is in the comprehension part that we start out, but as we follow Him, we become more competent.

Isn't it interesting also that in the Acts of the Apostles, when the disciples were persecuted, they were looked upon as "ignorant men"? **"They were unlearned and ignorant men ..."** (Acts 4:13 KJV). Then the verse goes on to say, **"they took knowledge of them, that they had been with Jesus."** They saw something of Jesus in these disciples. Christ had fulfilled the making process, but the making process was a continuous thing.

Hopefully, we are all growing spiritually. The moment we stop growing, we start dying. So we need to constantly follow Jesus.

Peter himself went through a lot of processes. In Acts, chapter 10, he had a revelation to go to the house of Cornelius; this revelation forced him to wrestle with some issues within himself regarding his own prejudice. God had to expose that to Peter, and then Peter drew the conclusion, **"God is no respecter of persons"** (Acts 10:34 KJV). Imagine Peter, who followed Christ and was a key person in the early Church, was still in the process of being made. So it's a continuous process.

Jesus said, **"Follow me, and I will make you ..."** (Matthew 4:19 KJV). To break that down, "Follow Me" is the comprehension part, and "I will make you" is a process of becoming competent to carry out that assignment.

The gap between comprehension and competency varies from person to person and from organization to organization. We are all on different levels of comprehension and competency. However, that gap doesn't have to stay a wide one. As we grow in preparing to do what God called us to do, we close that gap.

Jesus felt confident enough after three-and-a-half years

of ministry to say, **"Go and make disciples of all nations ..."** (Matthew 28:19). This means He had imparted to them, and now it was time for them to impact their world. Jesus made them competent over a period of time.

In Habakkuk, chapter 2, verses 1-3 KJV, the man of God saw the devastation of his people; and he sought God's face for an answer to their predicament.

"I will stand upon my watch, and set me upon the tower, and will watch to see what he will say unto me, and what I shall answer when I am reproved. And the Lord answered me, and said, Write the vision, and make it plain upon tables, that he may run that readeth it. For the vision is yet for an appointed time, but at the end it shall speak, and not lie: though it tarry, wait for it; because it will surely come, it will not tarry."

Four ways that visions can be obtained are:

- By illumination;

- By pursuit;

- By natural inclination; and

- By "accidental" discovery .

By Illumination

This is when God opens our eyes to His plan for us. Illumination is a personal revelation of an already existing truth or revelation. It is when the light bulb comes on. It is when something that was hidden

> *"Illumination is a personal revelation of an already existing truth or revelation."*

becomes uncovered to you.

In Galatians 1:15-16 KJV, the Apostle Paul refers to his encounter with God:

"**But when it pleased God, who separated me from my mother's womb, and called me by his grace, To reveal his Son in me, that I might preach him among the heathen; immediately I conferred not with flesh and blood.**"

In Isaiah chapter 60 verses 1 to 3 KJV we read:

"**Arise, shine; for thy light is come, and the glory of the Lord is risen upon thee. For, behold, the darkness shall cover the earth, and gross darkness the people: but the Lord shall arise upon thee, and his glory shall be seen upon thee. And the Gentiles shall come to thy light, and kings to the brightness of thy rising.**"

By Pursuit

The things of God do not come cheaply. They are not attained through a passive stance. We must actively pursue God to know Him in order to know His mind.

In Matthew 6:31-33 KJV Jesus said:

"**Therefore take no thought, saying, What shall we eat? or, What shall we drink? or, Wherewithal shall we be clothed? (For after all these things do the Gentiles seek:) for your heavenly Father knoweth that ye have need of all these things. But seek ye first the kingdom of God, and his righteousness; and all these things shall be added unto you.**"

Matthew 7:7-8 AMP states:

"**Keep on asking and it will be given you; keep**

on seeking and you will find; keep on knocking [reverently] and [the door] will be opened to you. For everyone who keeps on asking receives; and he who keeps on seeking finds; and to him who keeps on knocking, [the door] will be opened."

Then Psalm 42:1 KJV says, "**As the hart panteth after the water brooks, so panteth my soul after thee, O God.**"

By Natural Inclination

There may be some things that are already clear to you about your assignment and what you should be doing with your life. You may be naturally inclined to feed the poor, invent something that will help people, have ideas that naturally come to you, and a unique grace to help people. You do not need to be motivated, pushed, or forced to do it. It comes naturally to you. It may involve a special skill.

Many people take for granted the things they do naturally. These natural abilities may be a clue to your God-given assignment.

In Exodus chapter 31, God pointed out Bezaleel to Moses. Bezaleel was a man with the skill of craftsmanship and the ability to cut stones, carve timber to create great furniture etc. He had the advantage in that God's Spirit was clearly the source of these abilities. Can you identify those gifts and abilities that come naturally to you?

"Many people take for granted the things they do naturally. These natural abilities may be a clue to your God-given assignment."

By "Accidental" Discovery

There are no "accidents" in God. But sometimes we are

looking for one thing and find something else.

In Acts 9:1-6, we read of Paul's encounter on the road to Damascus. Paul contacted the high priest to get letters that would permit him to arrest believers in Christ and to bring them back captive to Jerusalem. Little did he know that he was about to be "set up" by the Lord Jesus. This encounter was initiated by God. By the time Christ worked out His plan in Paul, he became the greatest advocate for the faith he once sought to destroy.

In Exodus 3, Moses had an encounter with God that changed his life. He was tending the flock of Jethro his father-in-law when a strange sight distracted him. He looked to see why the bush was burning without being consumed. God then revealed his assignment to him.

Albert Einstein's father was an unsuccessful engineer. He gave five-year-old Albert his first compass. Little Albert was provoked and wondered why the compass arrow pointed north. This sparked his interest in the natural laws of physics. Albert Einstein's input into the field of physics sparked a flame for scientific explorations of the atom and the universe.

His mind did not get in the way of science, but created a way for science to tread. Some of his scientific discoveries were made simply by thinking them through. However, it all started when his father gave him a "toy compass."

In Summary

Principle: When we begin to know God, His heart and His vision are exposed. So to understand a vision, we must know God's heart and see from His point of view.

Four ways that visions can be obtained are:

•   By illumination;

- By pursuit;

- By natural inclination; and

- By "accidental" discovery.

SECTION V:
WHAT VISION DOES

CHAPTER 20
VISION RESTRAINS US

Proverbs 29, verse 18 NASB says, **"Where there is no vision, the people are unrestrained...."**

Many times when we talk about a lack of vision, people don't see the drastic outcome with their natural eyes. The effect on the people is that they are unrestrained, meaning undisciplined.

When you have a vision, it creates borders, boundaries, and a sense of focus. For example, light can be used in various ways. You can have light that floods a house, and you can have very focused light called a laser beam that can actually drill

> *"Vision restrains us, because it keeps us focused on the target."*

a hole in a solid object. So when a person lacks vision, he is not making any positive impact. The impact is not felt because there is no focus. Everything is haphazard. Vision restrains us, because it keeps us focused on the target.

Imagine an athlete training for four years just for one event in the Olympics. The athlete wakes and sleeps with a specific goal in mind. He or she says, "I'm not supposed to eat certain things that can make me less effective in training and preparing for my race." So they put certain precautions in place, which restrains or controls them, because they have a picture and an outcome in mind. That picture keeps them constrained. When you know what to say "yes" to, it makes saying "no" to the nonessentials much easier.

The Bible says, **"Looking unto Jesus, the author and finisher of our faith, who for the joy that was set before Him endured the cross, despising the shame, and has sat down at the right hand of the throne of God"** (Hebrews 12:2 NKJV). Jesus could have given up, but because of the picture of the end, He endured the cross and despised the shame.

Notice the phrase, **"Who for the joy that was set before Him ...."** There was something "set" or fixed before Him that stood as a guide or anchor. That joy that was set was so big that it swallowed up the suffering. That joy was the redemption of mankind from eternal damnation, making them citizens of God's Kingdom.

What joy is set before you? Your vision will create focus.

In Summary

Principle: When you have a vision, it creates borders, boundaries, and a sense of focus. Simply put, vision creates a disciplined life.

CHAPTER 21

VISION CREATES STRUCTURE

Once we have the big picture and it is clearly defined, we will become free from distractions and we will become more structured.

Daniel 1:3-5 (NIV) says this:

"Then the king ordered Ashpenaz, chief of his court officials, to bring into the king's service some of the Israelites from the royal family and the nobility – young men without any physical defect, handsome, showing aptitude for every kind of learning, well informed, quick to understand, and qualified to serve in the king's palace. He was to teach them the language and literature of the Babylonians. The king assigned them a daily amount of food and wine from the king's table. They were to be trained for three years, and after that they were to enter the king's service."

Food for Thought

Here we see a king who had structure. This king set a very high standard. The conclusion of his criteria was this: "No one could serve before this king if he did not meet the standards."

Now look down at verse 17 of Daniel, chapter 1: **"To these four young men God gave knowledge and understanding of all kinds of literature and learning. And Daniel could**

understand visions and dreams of all kinds."

This ungodly king set a standard and put a structure in place to meet his goal. Although he was not a God-fearing king, God got involved by blessing His children with the ability to fulfill every requirement set by the king.

If structure was not of God, God would not have given Daniel and his friends the things that He gave them. The structure created by the king put a demand on Daniel and his friends to seek God until they got a definite answer. They sought the face of God with specific requirements, because the king gave specific requirements. This is what vision does.

The king wanted Daniel and his friends to be trained in the learning of literature, so that is exactly what God gave them. God is a God of structure. It is not ungodly to have structure. It is not ungodly to have certain standards. Even though this was a secular king, God honored the standards he set because structure is a reflection of His nature.

In Summary

Principle: Structure creates a framework for unleashing creativity and places a demand on our potential. With structure, we can measure growth more accurately over a reasonable amount of time.

CHAPTER 22

VISION CREATES STABILITY AND ORDER

Stability and order are by-products of structure. Imagine a society without a certain structure. Even the legal system is a form of structure. The legal system is a vision to keep order in society so that its citizens are protected.

For example, we have a speed limit to protect each motorist from harming himself and others. Can you imagine if you got on the road and there were no speed limits? Worse yet, what if there were no law enforcement officers to ensure that everyone abides by the laws? There would be chaos. Simply put, the vision behind the speed limit is safety.

According to the Department of Transportation, Federal Highway Administration, in the year 2000, annual highway travel reached approximately 2.7 trillion miles driven by Americans.[1] From the Vision Statement of the Department of Transportation, you can conclude that their primary objective is safety.

When a vision is clearly given, there is a sense of expectation in the recipients, provided the vision has been cast correctly.

Mark 9:23 NJKV says, **"All things are possible to him who believes."** So when God begins to give a vision to you, something in you begins to say, "Okay, I am just going to spend

"Everything that God does operates on the principle of seedtime and harvest."

time with God, and I am going to trust God." You have an expectation.

Everything that God does operates on the principle of seedtime and harvest. The seed is the vision He gives, and with that seed comes the divine spark that stimulates faith for the harvest.

Vision also creates discipline. The impact of vision on your life is that it helps you to rearrange your priorities.

In Summary

Principle: Stability and order are by-products of structure. You cannot sustain a vision in an atmosphere of chaos.

CHAPTER 23
VISION CREATES MOTIVATION

Vision creates motivation, which is also linked to expectation. When you have a higher level of expectation, you become naturally motivated. This fact about vision also affects the people who are following us.

If a vision is not cast properly, the people won't be motivated. In other words, a vision should be cast so well that the people take ownership of it.

The language is not just, "Pastor says," but "This is what Pastor said and this is what we are doing." The people must be so motivated by the vision that they naturally feel a part of it. Once they understand the vision, you will not have to drive them. They will become self-motivated.

Every God-given vision requires God to fulfill it.

Lamentations 3:37 AMP declares, **"Who is he who speaks and it comes to pass, if the Lord has not authorized and commanded it?"** God's vision will lead to a desire to seek Him, the author and finisher of our faith.

As you look at several portions of scripture, you will see that God gives the vision and man himself may feel overwhelmed. We believe he should, because if it depended on him, he could get the glory; but if it depends on God, then God alone gets the glory.

In Summary

Principle 1: Vision creates motivation, which is also linked to expectation.

Principle 2: When you have a higher level of expectation, you become naturally motivated. This fact about vision also affects the people who are following us.

SECTION VI:
GETTING IT DONE

CHAPTER 24

THE POWER OF INSIGHT

In the pursuit of the fullness of human life, everything depends on this frame of reference, this habitual outlook, this basic vision that I have of myself, others, life, the world, and God. What we see is what we get. Consequently, if you or I are to change, to grow into persons who are more fully human and more fully alive, we shall certainly have to become aware of our vision and patiently work at redressing its imbalances and eliminating its distortions. All real and permanent growth must begin here. A shy person can be coaxed into assuming an air of confidence, but it will only be a mask—one mask replacing another. There can be no real change, no real growth in any of us until and unless our basic perception of reality, or vision, is changed. — John Powell[1]

But as it is written, Eye hath not seen, nor ear heard, neither have entered into the heart of man, the things which God hath prepared for them that love him. But God hath revealed them unto us by his Spirit: for the Spirit searcheth all things, yea, the deep things of God.

— (1 Corinthians 2:9,10 KJV)

Earlier we mentioned this principle: *every form of foresight begins with insight. Foresight is stifled or hindered when insight is shallow.*

Insight determines the amount of foresight. In other words, when you have insight on what God has revealed to you, it will help you to project ahead and then you can start implementing a strategy. The end result of this whole process determines the impact you will make.

This is my definition of the word "impact": Impact is made when you leave a place or people, and there is sufficient evidence present to show that you were there.

Every day of our lives we are making impact, whether positive or negative. So impact does not require insight. The question is: Do we have the desired impact that we want to make? It is possible that some of us may not know the impact we are making until thirty years from now.

My question to you: Is it possible to make impact without insight? The answer is "yes." The problem is that the impact will be chaotic and perhaps detrimental to you and others.

If you are building a house and you throw away the blueprint and just randomly build, you might end up with a house, but that house will be a mess. But when you build a house using insight as to where every room will be, the size of each room, etc., you can expect to reach your goal.

Lesson: Just like the house, insight is the blueprint of any vision. This insight must come from God (our Source).

Years ago we wrote a book titled, *The Progenitor Principle: Why You Must Leave a Legacy Behind*. We wrote it as sons reaching out to fathers, to look back at our generation so that they can infuse in us those things that are needed. The baton must be accurately passed on to the next generation.

While we were in Zimbabwe, one of the men who attended our meetings got a hold of the book. He read about halfway through the book before the next meeting. He came to us and said, "I see my mistake." He had a nineteen-year-old son.

He went on to say, "I made so many mistakes. I see it now." The impact was made over that nineteen-year period. The insight he gained in one day brought light to a mistake that had lingered for nineteen years! He was making impact in his son's life even though he lacked insight.

When we look around the world and take nation by nation or continent by continent, it becomes apparent which nations or continents have been governed by vision or a lack of it. As you look at the people, what do they aspire for? This is a clue that points to insight or chaos. Impact is made by action or inaction.

Have you seen the History Channel cover a story on a war zone? While you didn't actually see bombs going off, you can see the effects of war; demolished and bullet-ridden buildings are a sign that something devastating took place. You definitely can see the negative impact that has been made. The same is true of positive impact. It is tangible. You can see or perceive it. Sometimes it's even on the countenance of the people. There's something different. Every day we are making impact.

Principle: Impact is made when you leave a place or people, and there is sufficient evidence present to show that you were there.

Have you seen a dent in a wall made by a car? While the car was removed, the dent is still there. The car left its mark. The dent in the wall screams, "Something happened here!" All of us are leaving marks – negative or positive – every single day.

> *"Impact is made when you leave a place or people, and there is sufficient evidence present to show that you were there."*

Years ago I was on a plane and sat next to a banker.

We struck up a conversation, and he gave an example of a guy who was a crossing guard at his child's school. When the children got out of school, he put up the signs, stopped the traffic, and helped the children cross safely.

The banker and the crossing guard, an older man probably in his eighties, became friends. When the crossing guard died, the banker went to his funeral.

At the funeral, the banker noticed that no member of the deceased's family came to the podium to say anything. In fact, it appeared that no family members were present. He was shocked.

The banker found out later what had actually happened earlier in this man's life. He was a very ambitious man and had neglected his family. He had created strained relationships with his family, who in turn, wanted nothing to do with him.

In his latter years, he tried to correct the damage by adopting other people's children. He became very passionate about his duties and built relationships outside of his family. At his death, the impact of the damage to his family became very obvious.

Impact is made every day. Sometimes the fruit of our impact doesn't show up immediately.

I remember talking to the director of a pharmacy who appeared to be in his early fifties. As he talked, he lamented, "Here I am the director of a pharmacy. In my earlier years, I was so ambitious," and he related how his ambition had negatively impacted his family.

As I stated previously, sometimes our impact is not seen until years later.

Let's pray this prayer right now: *Lord, shine the spotlight on me, and show me where I am missing it. Help me, Lord."*

I remember when we were actively involved in a youth group in New York for four years. There was a very quiet young man who hardly said a word to us. He appeared to be an introvert.

Years later, when we returned and visited, he saw us and said to us, "You don't know the impact that you had on my life." We were stunned, because he never opened his mouth and never showed any positive sign that we made any difference in his life.

Jesus died and rose about two thousand years ago, and His impact is still being felt.

Another example of a person who had a great impact in American history in the 1860s was a man by the name of Abraham Lincoln.

Abraham Lincoln had a very low rating among the people during his presidency. However, historians now look back and rank him as one of the greatest presidents America has ever had.

Lincoln went through a lot of struggles – personal as well as in the governmental area. He had a vision to end slavery, but back then the people didn't favor him or his ideas. Many people now say, however, "Wow! That man was before his time." What he did has had a great impact on the United States today.

A good example of a biblical forerunner is John the Baptist. Often, forerunners are not celebrated until after they are gone.

Sometimes forerunners are tempted to think that they have missed it or they doubt their assignment, because even for the forerunner, the vision is unfolding. They might look back and say, "Did I really do what I was assigned to do?" John the Baptist asked Jesus, **"Are You the Coming One, or do we look for another?"** (Matthew 11:3 NKJV).

Jesus did something that was very impressive. Normally,

for the average person, this sort of doubt could have been a cause for offense. Jesus demonstrated maturity. John the Baptist had a question about Jesus' ministry, but when the messengers of John left, Jesus began to magnify the ministry of John. By doing this, Jesus was indirectly magnifying His own ministry.

God's Mission Statement

A mission statement is a statement that clearly expresses your reason or purpose for being, the path you use to accomplish it, and finally, what motivates you to do so. A good and complete mission statement contains the following three elements:

I. Purpose.

II. Value System.

III. Strategy.

God's Mission Statement is found in John 3:16 KJV **"For God so loved the world, that he gave his only begotten Son, that whosoever believeth in him should not perish, but have everlasting life."**

What is God's purpose? To save men. What is God's value, and how does He show His value? Jesus said, "God so loved the world." The value God has for the world is His love for it revealed by giving His only begotten Son as our Substitute so we can have everlasting life. God's strategy: giving Jesus.

In summary, God has a value system: love for the world. God has a purpose: the salvation of man. God had a strategy: sending Jesus.

I can look at any mission statement and tell if it is a complete mission statement by looking at these same elements. We teach on how to write a compelling mission statement, for more information on downloading the message, visit vflm.org and obtain the two-part message: **"4 Big Myths 7 Great Facts about your Life's Mission."** Someone can look at our mission statement who has never met us and say, "Okay, I can see what this group or individual is about."

In Summary

Principle: Impact is made when you leave a place or people, and there is sufficient evidence present to show that you were there.

CHAPTER 25

EXECUTION: GETTING IT DONE

"One of the most important qualities of a change agent is the ability to take responsibility. Nothing changes until someone takes responsibility for change."

– Olumide Taiwo

...Moses was divinely instructed when he was about to make the tabernacle. For He said, "See that you make all things according to the pattern shown you on the mountain."

— (Hebrews 8:5 NKJV).

"The tragedy of life is not that it ends so soon, but that we wait so long to begin it" – W. M. Lewis.

An example in scripture of the execution of a God-given assignment is found in the life of Nehemiah.

In Nehemiah 1:7-9 KJV, Nehemiah states the condition of the hearts of the Israelites:

"We have dealt very corruptly against thee, and have not kept the commandments, nor the statutes, nor the judgments, which thou commandedst thy servant Moses. Remember, I beseech thee, the word

that thou commandedst thy servant Moses, saying, If ye transgress, I will scatter you abroad among the nations: But if ye turn unto me, and keep my commandments, and do them; though there were of you cast out unto the uttermost part of the heaven, yet will I gather them from thence, and will bring them unto the place that I have chosen to set my name there."

The Assignment

Nehemiah 2:11-12 KJV says:

"So I came to Jerusalem, and was there three days. And I arose in the night, I and some few men with me; neither told I any man what my God had put in my heart to do at Jerusalem: neither was there any beast with me, save the beast that I rode upon."

While Nehemiah's task was to rebuild the ruined walls of Jerusalem, we should ask ourselves, "what are we called to build"? What are we building? Our prayer should be, *Lord, give me the kind of clarity You gave to Nehemiah who awakened from slumber after decades of decay. And, Lord, show me treasures, as You express in Isaiah 45:1-3 KJV:*

"Thus saith the Lord to his anointed, to Cyrus, whose right hand I have holden, to subdue nations before him; and I will loose the loins of kings, to open before him the two leaved gates; and the gates shall not be shut; I will go before thee, and make the crooked places straight: I will break in pieces the gates of brass, and cut in sunder the bars of iron: And I will give thee the treasures of darkness, and hidden riches of secret places, that thou mayest know that I, the Lord, which call thee by thy name, am the God of Israel."

Nehemiah had a heart for God's people, and in Nehemiah 1:2 KJV he made a heartfelt inquiry: **"That Hanani, one of my brethren, came, he and certain men of Judah; and I asked them concerning the Jews that had escaped, which were left of the captivity, and concerning Jerusalem."**

Are we sensitive to people around us? Nehemiah asked the question because he was sensitive to the plight of his people, and he had a real love for his people.

Nehemiah prayed to God on behalf of Israel, and the cause of devastation and captivity became clear. We can be going on for decades and not know why things are not working. Until we get clarity from on High, the struggling will continue. As it has been said, *faith begins where the will of God is known.*

Divine Empowerment to Follow Through

Romans 8:26-27 KJV says that the Holy Spirit within us groans as He makes intercession for us according to the will of God. It is He, the Holy Spirit, who will empower and guide us in the fulfilment of the vision and assignment:

"Likewise the Spirit also helpeth our infirmities: for we know not what we should pray for as we ought: but the Spirit itself maketh intercession for us with groanings which cannot be uttered. And he that searcheth the hearts knoweth what is the mind of the Spirit, because he maketh intercession for the saints according to the will of God."

Order our steps, Lord: **"Establish my steps and direct them by [means of] Your word; let not any iniquity have dominion over me"** (Psalm 119:133 AMP).

Elizabeth filled with the Holy Spirit spoke prophetically to Mary:

And blessed is she that believed: for there shall be a performance of those things which were told her from the Lord. — (Luke 1:45 KJV).

God has not called us to perform. He has called us to participate. We participate by believing and following through with God's instructions. He performs by making the humanly impossible, possible.

A lot of things are happening in the world. The questions we should be asking are:

• What is happening inside of us?

• Who is leading us – the reigning trends in society or God's agenda?

First Samuel 2:3-4,9 KJV says this:

"Talk no more so exceeding proudly; let not arrogancy come out of your mouth: for the Lord is a God of knowledge, and by him actions are weighed. The bows of the mighty men are broken, and they that stumbled are girded with strength...He will keep the feet of his saints, and the wicked shall be silent in darkness; for by strength shall no man prevail."

Zechariah 4:6 KJV lets us know that it is by the Spirit of God that our assignments will be fulfilled:

"Then he answered and spake unto me, saying, This is the word of the Lord unto Zerubbabel, saying, Not by might, nor by power, but by my spirit, saith the Lord of hosts."

Unless we are guided by God's Spirit, our efforts are in vain, as Psalm 127:1-2 KJV says:

"Except the Lord build the house, they labour in

vain that build it: except the Lord keep the city, the watchman waketh but in vain. It is vain for you to rise up early, to sit up late, to eat the bread of sorrows: for so he giveth his beloved sleep."

Nehemiah was a man that God had prepared for the hour. After getting insight from God about what to do and receiving favor from the King, he embarked on a very long journey.

Look again at this statement: Nehemiah 2:11 KJV says:

"So I came to Jerusalem...." Without an in-depth study, it is easy to miss how important this statement is. Nehemiah traveled from Persia. The distance between Shushan (Persia or present day Iran) and Jerusalem is over one thousand miles!

To give perspective look at Ezra who made a similar trip before Nehemiah. Unlike Nehemiah who came to Jerusalem from Persia (in present day Iran), Ezra traveled from Babylon (near present day Iraq). While Iran and Iraq are neighboring countries, the distance between Iraq and Jerusalem is closer than the distance between Iran and Jerusalem.

Ezra 7:6-9 (KJV):

"This Ezra went up from Babylon; and he was a ready scribe in the law of Moses, which the Lord God of Israel had given: and the king granted him all his request, according to the hand of the Lord his God upon him. And there went up some of the children of Israel, and of the priests, and the Levites, and the singers, and the porters, and the Nethinims, unto Jerusalem, in the seventh year of Artaxerxes the king. And he came to Jerusalem in the fifth month, which was in the seventh year of the king. For upon the first day of the first month began he to go up from Babylon, and on the first day of the fifth month came he to Jerusalem, according to the good hand of his

God upon him."

It took Ezra and his team four months to reach their destination. That is commitment.

Nehemiah must have had a similar experience in his travel. Because he was set on accomplishing his God-given vision, distance was not an issue.

> *"The question that begs to be asked from you and me is, 'How far are we willing to travel to fulfill our God-given vision?'"*

The question that begs to be asked from you and me is, "How far are we willing to travel to fulfill our God- given vision?"

We cannot just talk about the vision; we must step out in faith and do what God has called us to do. You may have a leading in the arena of business, or government, or media, arts and entertainment, education, the family or the Church. The important thing is to step out as God prompts you. Take practical steps to fulfil the vision. You can register a domain name, and build a website. You can write a book. The list goes on.

The progression of positive impact begins with insight. Insight begets foresight. When foresight is coupled with implementation, the result is impact.

In Summary

Principle 1: One of the single most important qualities of a change agent is the ability to take responsibility. Nothing changes until someone takes responsibility for change.

Principle 2: We cannot just talk about the vision; we must step out in faith and do what God has called us to do.

CHAPTER 26

TWO STANDARDS OF EXCELLENCE?

Can there be two standards of excellence: one for the so-called developed countries and another for the developing nations?

The truth is, the standards we set are a result of how we see ourselves. In the introduction we stated that Africa is a rich continent. We could add one more positive observation about Africa; as a continent it has great weather year round unlike the West that tackles extreme cold during portions of the year. This means there are more days in a year to make the continent of Africa the most productive, and advanced continent the world has ever seen. What an advantage!

So why is Africa as a continent virtually behind on almost every scale measuring development? If it is rich in natural resources and has conducive weather year round, why does it lag behind?

The Root Philosophies of the West versus that of Africa

While the following may be an oversimplification of the reasons why other continents thrive and most of Africa doesn't, it serves as a thought provoking analysis to help us develop a forward thinking mindset.

The Western nations are rooted in Greek philosophy, while historically most African countries were largely rooted in superstition and a lack of investigation. This is huge; it has been said that a tree is only as good as its roots. While Greek philosophy is not Bible-based and elevates knowledge as supreme, it has one distinct positive characteristic: it questions why things are the way they are, and seeks to find how things can improve. This was the predominant foundational philosophy of the West. On the other hand, superstition accepts cultural norms at face value, embraces traditions, and even accepts assumptions passed along from generation to generation.

The Little Girl and the Pot Roast

The story of the pot roast illustrates the point with irrefutable clarity. While making a pot roast, a young girl notices that her mother cuts off certain portions of meat and throws them away. Curious, she asks her mum, "why did you cut off those pieces and throw them away?" Her mum did not have an answer but was lucky that the little girl's grandmother was there. So the little girl's mum told her to ask her grandmother. Surprisingly, her grandmother did not know; but luckily for the little girl her great- grandmother was present. Here is where her curiosity paid off; her great- grandmother had the answer. Her great-grandmother said, "Honey, I don't know why your mum, and grandmother cut off portions of the pot roast. I cut off portions of mine because my pot was too small."

"It is worse when leaders who have been enlightened, have traveled the world, and have become well educated, maintain systems of mediocrity."

The lesson here is that traditions are good, but it is better to understand why. By asking a question, the little girl effectively ended a needless tradition by getting to the root cause.

Now imagine the underlying philosophies governing developed nations and that of the underdeveloped continent of Africa. If you live based on traditions that are neither questioned nor tested, you may live beneath your potential. It is worse when leaders who have been enlightened, have traveled the world, and have become well educated, maintain systems of mediocrity.

Why has Africa suffered the atrocities of bad leaders and even dictatorship? Why has unchecked corruption thrived? To advance, you must ask questions.

Lack of Value for Time

I remember a humorous event that happened a few years ago. It was eye-opening. My wife and I attended a birthday party for the child of a family friend who happens to be African. She told her American friends to come to the party at 2 pm but told her African friends to come at 12 noon. Everyone arrived at the same time! Understanding how Africans view time, she decided to tell her African friends to arrive much earlier knowing that they would be late.

The West takes time more literally and adheres to a culture of timeliness, unlike Africans who mostly are culturally entrenched in a value system that devalues punctuality. The underlying implication here is this: if you do not value time you cannot maximize what it has to offer.

"The underlying implication here is this: if you do not value time you cannot maximize what it has to offer."

Psalm 90 verse 12 (KJV): **"So teach us to number our days, that we may apply our hearts unto wisdom."**

The writer implies that teaching would lead to application.

Application involves taking initiative. Proverbs 6:6-11 (MSG):

> "....look at an ant. Watch it closely; let it teach you a thing or two. Nobody has to tell it what to do. All summer it stores up food; at harvest it stockpiles provisions. So how long are you going to laze around doing nothing? How long before you get out of bed? A nap here, a nap there, a day off here, a day off there, sit back, take it easy—do you know what comes next? Just this: You can look forward to a dirt-poor life, poverty your permanent houseguest!"

In Summary

Principle 1: With regards to a culture of excellence, the standards we set are a result of how we see ourselves.

Principle 2: If you live your life based on traditions that are neither questioned nor tested, you may be living beneath your potential.

Principle 3: If you do not value time you cannot maximize the benefits time has to offer.

CHAPTER 27
THE FORERUNNER PRINCIPLE: A MULTIPLICATION FACTOR

There are certain names that have gone down in history and are synonymous with a daring feat or outstanding accomplishment. When you mention the name Michelangelo, thoughts of outstanding paintings fill the mind. The name Beethoven stimulates thoughts of a melodious symphony. The Wright brothers conjure thoughts of defying gravity. Anywhere you go the name Albert Einstein is synonymous with sheer genius. Regardless of the field of endeavor, these individuals have left a mark that cannot be erased. They will live forever in the annals of history.

Among the many outstanding individuals that have graced the earth is a man by the name William Wilberforce. Wilberforce was a strong antagonist of the institution of slavery, and fought for many grueling years to see it abolished. Even though he suffered a number of defeats, which spanned a period of twenty years, he pressed on to see his heart's yearning realized. In 1807 after two decades, he experienced his first success when a bill was passed to abolish the slave trade in the British West Indies. Although a step in the right direction, "this statute, however, did not change the legal position of persons enslaved before its enactment..."[1]

Several years prior to the enactment of this statute, John Wesley had written an encouraging letter that proved to be of great help to Wilberforce:

> **Unless the divine power has raised you up... I see not how you can go through your glorious enterprise in opposing that execrable villainy, which is the scandal of religion, of England, and of human nature....O be not weary of well doing! Go on, in the name of God in the power of His might, till even American slavery (the vilest that ever saw the sun) shall vanish away before it.**

Wilberforce persisted till the end. He became the forerunner to the emancipation of slaves and the abolishment of slavery. In 1834, a year after his death, 800,000 slaves, mostly in the British West Indies were set free.

What Forerunners Do

Etymology or root meaning of the word 'forerunner': Prodromos, an adjective signifying "running forward, going in advance," is used as a noun, of "those who were sent before to take observations," acting as scouts, especially in military matters...In the NT it is said of Christ in Hebrews 6:20, as going in advance of His followers who are to be where He is, when He comes to receive them to Himself. In the Sept., Number 13:21, "forerunners (of the grape)"; Isa. 28:4, "an early (fig)." (Vine's Complete Expository Dictionary).

So forerunners are "those who are sent before to take observations." This is so crucial. Why? Because 'how' they see what they see determines 'what' they report back. Literally, the forerunner is the 'animated CD player' for the one he precedes. In essence, he sets the tone!

A forerunner is also synonymous with the word foretoken. A foretoken is simply something that serves as a sign of future happenings. This means a forerunner does not provide a full picture, but is simply a glimpse of what is to come. Another related word is advertiser. Oftentimes, we see an ad before we handle the product. The forerunner is an announcer.

The forerunner is the first person one comes in contact with, and then one meets the person he precedes. He (the forerunner) sets the stage for the one to come after. From a position of timing and sequence, the forerunner appears to be more significant than the one he goes ahead of. However, when the one who emerges after him comes on the scene, the forerunner's main assignment is now over. It is important to note: the forerunner is a part of something much greater than himself.

> *"...the forerunner is a part of something much greater than himself."*

For the generations to come, we are forerunners. Our legacy is the impact we leave behind; whether it be positive or negative.

Ironically, while John the Baptist was Jesus' forerunner, as far as the second coming of Christ is concerned, we are His forerunners. So it is absolutely crucial we do our parts well. Jesus is the forerunner to the Church (Hebrews 6:20). Notice in John 14:12 (KJV):

"Verily, verily, I say unto you, He that believeth on me, the works that I do shall he do also; and greater works than these shall he do; because I go unto my Father."

Jesus applied the forerunner principle in this passage above. Since he preceded His Church, He made sure that the Church would be able to do greater works than He did.

The forerunner principle indicates that the forerunner's mission is to create an atmosphere conducive for the operation and multiplying impact for what will come after. So the whole idea is to create a path that makes it easier for the one who is to come: both quantitatively and qualitatively.

I am convinced that our leaders, teachers, mentors, parents and ancestors are our forerunners. They either succeeded or failed in creating a path of life for us to tread. All things being equal, we ought to demonstrate better results than did our predecessors.

John the Baptist was the forerunner of Jesus. He understood his role very well. John the Baptist said that Jesus must "increase" and he (John) must "decrease" (John 3:30).

This increase is not addition, but a multiplying effect, the result of which is the Church.

When the forerunner principle is not correctly applied, there are adverse consequences. Adam gave less to Cain and Abel than what God initially entrusted into his hand. The result was not a multiplication of a God-given potential in its accurate form. Rather, it was passing on a seed of obscurity that has left the human race confused as it searches for meaning. Adam was made in the image of God. Seth, Adam's son (see Genesis 5:1-7), inherited the image of Adam. Adam gave less to Seth than God's original investment.

"When you play the role of a visionary figure to someone, you are initiating a multiplication factor. Something that you have is multiplied in something that someone else does."

God's intention was that Adam (in the unblemished state) multiply a reflection of himself, which was an accurate representation of God. This means there would have been a multitude of accurate representatives in the earth. Look at what men have been able to accomplish down through the centuries in the fallen state. Imagine if man had never sinned!

There is something here that we must catch. When you play the role of a visionary figure to someone, you are initiating a multiplication factor. Something that you have is multiplied in something that someone else does. If only potential mentors saw this! They would be able to successfully live beyond their own generation by the effects they have on their protégés.

In the book, The Millionaire Mind by Dr. Thomas J. Stanley, he writes about a true story that is both fascinating yet demonstrates the forerunner principle with irrefutable clarity. He writes about two fighter pilots that were distinguished during the Second World War:

> **Both of the pilots who "did it differently" were more than aces (see Raymond F. Toliver and Trevor J. Constable, The Blond Knight of Germany [Blue Ridge Summit, PA: Aero Books, 1970]). One, Major Erich Hartmann, is known in military literature as the Ace of Aces. He had 352 confirmed in-air victories. The other pilot who had the same unique strategy was Sergeant "Paule" Rossmann, Hartmann's mentor. He himself had more than 80 victories.**

> **It was Rossmann who invented the approach that ultimately led to Hartmann's extraordinary success. Early in his career, Rossmann suffered an injury to his arm that never healed, and he was unable to dogfight. In a typical dogfight, victory goes to those with superior physical strength. Rossmann knew he could never survive this kind of battle, so he developed a compensating technique. Substituting a much more calculating method for the macho dogfighting strategy, he carefully planned each and every attack. He spent much more time analyzing**

various targets of opportunity than actually firing bullets at his quarry. He attacked only when he was in the best possible position to win. Then he would focus all of his resources at the ideal target----the one that would give him the maximum return on his investment. Hartmann credits Rossmann's approach, the "see and decide prior to firing" method, with his own success. It also explains how Hartmann survived 1,425 combat missions, yet he was never even wounded.[2]

Wherever Hartmann is revered today in the annals of history, his mentor, Rossmann, will also be remembered as a noted contributor to Hartmann's distinguished successful in-air victories.

> *"We were designed to be multipliers, not just managers!"*

Our leaders are our forerunners; in turn, we become leaders who magnify what we are taught. What is entrusted to us must be multiplied not just maintained. We were designed to be multipliers, not just managers!

Elijah, the prophet was anointed, while Elisha, his protégé, had a double portion. (The word protégé means: one who is protected, trained, or guided by an influential person (Merriam-Webster Dictionary).

In Matthew 25 verse 14-28 the Master was enraged that one of his servants hid his talent. He expected to see increase. Why? Because things ought to be on the increase! That is the take away from this parable told by Jesus.

Principle: The lesser is blessed by the greater (Hebrews 7:7). And to be blessed is to be empowered to succeed.

This means you don't degenerate into less than you started out with. Neither do you simply maintain what you have been entrusted with. Instead, you excel beyond your starting point.

The results I produce should be easier and better than that of my forerunner.

Fathers are supposed to deposit into their children; ideally, children should magnify what they have been taught.

The four lepers in 2 Kings 7:3-20 were instrumental in the fulfillment of prophecy (see 2 Kings 7:1). Yet, everything that was set in motion started with a question: "Why...?" There was famine in besieged Samaria. The lepers asked themselves a very vital question. This question determined whether they stayed where they were and perished with the masses or rose to prominence as part of the solution. They asked in 2 Kings 7:3, "...Why sit here until we die?" This important question began their quest for change. They went to the enemy's camp where God had supernaturally provided abundance of food. They ate and drank till they were satisfied. While the lepers were first consumed by a desire to survive the famine, they made a shift in their focus to the rest of the people who suffered the same plight. It all started out with them wanting their own needs met; but the story does not conclude there. They decided to think beyond their own needs. The provision they received, became Samaria's supply. They were forerunners to the abundance later enjoyed by all!

"What comes after must have a greater effect than what preceded it: quantitatively and qualitatively. It is a multiplying effect! This is the principle of the forerunner."

The result: What comes after must have a greater effect than what preceded it: quantitatively and qualitatively. It is a multiplying effect! This is the principle of the forerunner.

While it is true that there is no abiding success without a successor, the real success is not just finding a replacement. It is creating a path that ensures your successor will even do greater than you did. Any result falling short of this is a form of failure.

The challenge to this generation is this: Will we follow God's strategy to fulfill our destiny? Will we live the vision guided life?

In Summary

Principle 1: The forerunner principle indicates that the forerunner's mission is to create an atmosphere conducive for the operation and multiplying impact of those who will come after him or her.

Principle 2: The Forerunner is a part of something much greater than himself.

CHAPTER 28

OVERCOMING OBSTACLES IN LIFE

The day seemed long and dreary as the darkness had just begun. The sky was blue in its darkest form, and the very atmosphere suggested gloom and uncertainty. It was upon this fateful day in October that I made my way across town to see the house where I had lived many years ago. For some reason, I was uncertain if my state of mind was sensible or an expression of insanity at its peak. With the machismo I was able to engender, I marched forward toward the house of doom. I say doom because, ever since I left that house, prosperity of soul has been mine.

The time seemed to be at a stand still as I drove past several blocks. The lights from those houses were so radiant that the thought of Christmas crossed my mind. While I pondered my predicament I was interrupted by darkness as I approached the old cold house. The very sight of it making my heart skip a beat.

Upon getting to the house, I stepped out of the car and beheld what seemed to be a beautiful wooden finish---the door. However, as I approached the door the truth was made known. A feast of termites had ravaged it. As I made my way into the house, I was stunned as I heard the windows shatter and the old piano began to play without a pianist. I was about to run out of the house when I remembered who I was (a Christian with a mighty God whom the forces of evil could not withstand); and with a mighty voice I exclaimed, 'In the name of Jesus, peace be still.' Where there was once darkness, light now prevailed; where the icy hand of death conquered, the life of God permeated. There was an inner peace that surpasses all human understanding. Upon that thought, I woke up and discovered I had been dreaming. However, Jesus the Christ gained new respect in my heart that day.

At the heart of this story, we see that things are not always what they appear to be. Circumstances usually look more complicated than they really are. The fears we often experience are usually based on imagined realities. We invent an illusion that becomes real to us. Sometimes however, we actually face real circumstances that seem to stretch us to the limit. While perception determines response, response determines outcome.

"While perception determines response, response determines outcome."

In 1st Samuel chapter one, we read the story of Hannah. She was married to Elkanah. Elkanah had two wives: Hannah and Peninnah. Unlike Peninnah who had children, Hannah was barren. To say the least, Hannah was ridiculed by Peninnah and wept sorely. One day Hannah goes to the temple to pray. While there, she pours out her heart to God in distress. In the course of praying, she cries out to God; verse 11 states, **"...O LORD of hosts, if thou wilt indeed look on the affliction of thine handmaid, and remember me, and not forget thine** handmaid, but wilt give unto thine handmaid a man child, then I will give him unto the LORD all the days of his life, and there shall no razor come upon his head."

Eli saw her mouth moving as she prayed and thought she was drunk; so he confronted her. She told the priest her distress and what she was praying for. He gave her his blessing. Later on, she becomes pregnant and Samuel is born. Note: we do not hear anything else about Peninnah or her children after chapter one. Yet,

> *"Your end in life is not always determined by how you start out. Your faith in God can catapult you out of obscurity into prominence...."*

Samuel becomes one of the most prominent figures in the book. In fact, the book is named after him. It proves this point: Your end in life is not always determined by how you start out. Your faith in God can catapult you out of obscurity into prominence (not for vain show but for positive impact to your generation).

You may have come from a dysfunctional home. Your father may have been absent, leaving your mother or perhaps your grandparents to raise you. You may feel unwanted, rejected, and despised. The very fact that you exist is testimony to your importance on this planet.

God is in the business of taking nothing and creating something good out of it.

When he was seven years old, his family was forced out of their home on a legal technicality, and he had to work to help support them. At age nine, his mother died. At 22, he lost his job as a store clerk. He wanted to go to law school, but his education wasn't good enough. At 23, he went into debt to become a partner in a small store. At 26, his business partner

died, leaving him a huge debt that took years to repay. At 28, after courting a girl for four years, he asked her to marry him. She said no. At 37, on his third try he was elected to Congress, but two years later, he failed to be reelected. At 41, his four-year-old son died. At 45, he ran for the Senate again, and lost. At 47, he failed as the vice-presidential candidate. At 49, he ran for the Senate again, and lost. At 51, he was elected president of the United States. His name was Abraham Lincoln, a man many consider the greatest leader the country ever had. Some people get all the breaks.[1]

In Hebrews 12:2,3 we read,

"Looking unto Jesus the author and finisher of our faith; who for the joy that was set before him endured the cross, despising the shame, and is set down at the right hand of the throne of God. For consider him that endured such contradiction of sinners against himself, lest ye be wearied and faint in your minds."

> "The adversities may originally be designed to hinder us. However, with God we cannot be hindered."

Human perception is often flawed. We see many people who have faced insurmountable odds rise to impact humanity. All of us will face adverse circumstances at one point in our lives. These circumstances will try to convince us that we are not capable of fulfilling our God-given destinies. The adversities may originally be designed to hinder us. However, with God we cannot be hindered.

Some of the world's greatest men and women have been saddled with disabilities and adversities but have managed to overcome them. Cripple him, and you have a Sir Walter Scott. Lock him in a prison cell, and you have a John Bunyan. Bury him in the snows of Valley Forge, and you have a George Washington. Raise him in abject poverty, and you have an Abraham Lincoln. Subject him to bitter religious prejudice, and you have a Benjamin Disraeli. Strike him down with infantile paralysis, and he becomes a Franklin D. Roosevelt. Burn him so severely in a schoolhouse fire that the doctors say he will never walk again, and you have a Glenn Cunningham, who set a World's record in 1934 for running a mile in 4 minutes, 6.7 seconds. Deafen a genius composer, and you have a Ludwig van Beethoven. Have him or her born black in a society filled with racial discrimination, and you have a Booker T. Washington, a Harriet Tubman, a Marian Anderson, or a George Washington Carver. Make him the first child to survive in a poor Italian family of eighteen children, and you have an Enrico Caruso. Have him born of parents who survived a Nazi concentration camp, paralyze him from the waist down when he is four, and you have an incomparable concert violinist, Itzhak Perlman. Call him a slow learner, retarded, and write him off as ineducable, and you have Albert Einstein.[2]

These individuals all faced the impossible. They were confronted with the challenges of life. They defied the norm and rose to make their contributions to humanity. From the distant land of Leningrad to Lagos, from Lagos to Lexington, and from the pyramids of Egypt to Rome, we appreciate the artistic works of artists who have come and gone. Names like Michelangelo and Rembrandt come to mind. As we behold their works, we marvel at the brilliance that these men were able to demonstrate through outstanding artistic abilities.

Yet the truth remains: 'No outstanding portrait has ever come about by the random strokes of a brush on canvas without a vision of the outcome.' The same truth applies to our lives. We cannot allow our lives to be lived randomly without cause. You cannot affect humanity positively without a positive cause. We must prayerfully search the word of God to know our assignment and strengthen our resolve. Why? When we find our place and function there, though opposition may come (and it will), its effect will be minimized by our God given resolve.

2 Timothy 2: 3 states **"Thou therefore endure hardness, as a good soldier of Jesus Christ."**

"God's Word is our source of Faith and Truth."

Fear paralyses potential. We are at our lowest level of potential when we are paralysed by fear. Fear is a big exaggerator. It often invents circumstances that are really barriers in our minds. Once we can get past those barriers, we see the truth. God's Word is our source of Faith and Truth. It gives us the understanding necessary to live a life of courage.

Perspective is everything. When your perspective is messed up, your response to life will be messed up! Do you know that most misunderstandings are based on wrong perspectives?

We need to be people of courage. We are on the verge of change, the dawning of a new day. Those things man has not mastered he fears. The Bible says, "I am the LORD, I do not change." In the natural, change is the only constant in life; supernaturally speaking, God never changes. If we will fulfill destiny in these evil days, we will definitely have to rest on the God who never changes.

It is not unreasonable to assume that in the 21st century man will come up with the most impressive, breathtaking inventions we have ever known. It is also safe to assume that what the future holds with regard to technology will make the 20th century pale in comparison. We will see man rise in his creative abilities without regard for the God who endowed him with those abilities in the first place. Consequently, there will be a multiplicity of gods that will arise as man bows down at the altar of his corrupt inventions. Morality will become obsolete to many. This is the verdict of the Bible on these last days. You might conclude that this is our current reality today. You are right. However, Jesus Christ is coming for the Church, a glorious Church. The Church of Jesus is His body on the earth. It is the vehicle through which He has chosen to express Himself on the earth. As the world gets worse, we must be at our best.

It is no longer time to sit by and be vague concerning what God has called us to do. We must take a hold of our purpose on this earth and leave a mark that cannot be erased. Apostle Paul was a man that knew opposition on all fronts, yet his resolve to do what God called him to do is mind-boggling.

Paul declares in Phil 3:12-15 (AMPLIFIED BIBLE):

"...but I press on to lay hold of (grasp and make my own, that for which Christ Jesus (the Messiah) has laid hold of me and made me His own. I do not consider, brethren, that I have captured and made it my own [yet]; but one thing I do [it is my one aspiration]: forgetting what lies behind and straining to what lies ahead. I press on toward the goal to win the [supreme and heavenly] prize to which God in Christ Jesus is calling us upward. So let those [of us] who are spiritually mature and full-grown have this mind and hold these convictions; and if in any respect you have a different attitude of mind, God will make that clear to you also."

> *"One of the most important things we will ever learn in life is the ability to forget. Many of us are trapped by what happened in our past, be it positive or negative."*

One of the most important things we will ever learn in life is the ability to forget. Many of us are trapped by what happened in our past, be it positive or negative. We need to forget our past successes or we will never know the joy of new accomplishments for God. Yet, we need to forget our past failures or they will rob us of the ability to venture into the unknown. For Christians, the future holds promise; we will be with the Lord Jesus Christ for eternity. However, while we are here, we have a job to do. There are countless millions waiting for us to show up and deliver what God has invested in us! As we analyze the above scripture closely, we see something peculiar about Paul's statement. He was determined to lay a hold of something. What was it? The answer can be seen in verse 12. Paul was determined to grasp the very thing Christ had in mind when He grabbed a hold of him (Paul).

> *"God is more concerned with us knowing and fulfilling His will than we are in finding out what it is."*

But wait a minute. How can you grasp a hold of something if you do not know what that thing is? We must spend time with God and follow our hearts as the Holy Spirit begins to give us direction. It seems a lot of people spend half their lives trying to discover the will of God, and then by the time they find it, time has run out. What a shame! I strongly believe that discovering the will of God for our lives is not as complicated as many have made it. First of all, look into the Word of God. God is more concerned with us knowing and fulfilling His will than we are in finding out what it is.

Look at Paul's prayer in Colossians chapter 1 verses 9,10 (AMPLIFIED BIBLE):

"For this reason we also, from the day we heard of it, have not ceased to pray and make [special] request for you, [asking] that you may be filled with the full (deep and clear) knowledge of His will in all spiritual wisdom [in comprehensive insight into the ways and purposes of God] and in understanding and discernment of spiritual things—That you may walk (live and conduct yourselves) in a manner worthy of the Lord, fully pleasing to Him and desiring to please Him in all things, bearing fruit in every good work and steadily growing and increasing in and by the knowledge of God [with fuller, deeper, and clearer insight, acquaintance, and recognition]."

God's desire for us is that we have a spiritual intelligence that makes us apt where His will is concerned. This intelligence does not come about by secular education, but is acquired through illumination of the Spirit of God. God begins to give us comprehensive insight into His ways. Not only will we know His will, we will know how to implement it when the occasion arises; that is where spiritual intelligence comes in.

Many of us do not fail in knowing what to do, we fail in the 'how to do it' aspect! We need to pray these prayers in Colossians for ourselves constantly, and see God move on our behalf. Or else, how can we fulfill His will if we are ignorant as to what His will is?

As we receive marching orders from God, we should be careful not to confuse obstacles with a lack of purpose. That is, do not determine whether or not you are doing God's will by the challenges or opposition you receive. The truth remains, 'whether or not you fulfill your purpose in life, opposition is bound to come your way.' However, with the help of God we can make apostle Paul's declaration our own: **"I have strength for all things in Christ Who empowers me [I am ready for anything and equal to anything through Him Who infuses inner strength into me; I am self-sufficient in Christ's sufficiency]."** (Philippians 4:13 AMP).

In Summary

Principle 1: The fears we often experience are usually based on imagined realities.

Principle 2: Perception determines response; response determines outcome.

Principle 3: With God nothing can hinder us.

Principle 4: Fear paralyses potential.

Principle 5: Do not confuse obstacles with a lack of purpose.

Principle 6: Your end in life is not always determined by how you start out. Your faith in God makes all the difference.

CHAPTER 29
COURAGE IS NOT AN ACT!

It is not the critic who counts; not the man who points out how the strong man stumbles, or where the doer of deeds could have done them better. The credit belongs to the man who is actually in the arena, whose face is marred by dust and sweat and blood; who strives valiantly; who errs, and comes short again and again, because there is not effort without error and shortcoming; but who does actually strive to do the deeds; who knows the great enthusiasms, the great devotions; who spends himself in a worthy cause; who at best knows in the end the triumphs of high achievement and who at the worst, if he fails, at least fails while daring greatly, so that his place shall never be with those cold and timid souls who know neither victory nor defeat.

— **Theodore Roosevelt** [1]

If you see a person on television once or twice, does this make him or her a television celebrity? How about a man who played in his soccer team when he was in school, does this make him a professional soccer star? A person assembles an electrical appliance; does this make him an electrician? The answers to these questions seem obvious, and to conclude in the affirmative would be absurd. Yet, in other areas of life that demand action, we are too quick to conclude things based on our perception.

Just like our examples above, courage is not an act! Courage is a mindset and lifestyle based on understanding.

There may be an *act* of courage with little or no understanding, but there never is a *life* of courage void of it. A life of courage exemplifies consistency. An act of courage may never be reproduced again. It is just like giving to a charity; one generous act of giving does not make you a benevolent person, likewise, an act of courage or courageous deed does not stamp on you the emblem of bravery.

If courage is a mindset based on understanding in a given area or subject, it follows that true courage is consistent. When we lack consistency in an area in our lives it can be linked to a lack of understanding or the failure to take responsibility for what we do know.

> *"...courage is the result of a lifestyle that has embraced knowledge in the arena it finds itself."*

Courage is a by-product of a deep-rooted understanding. Put slightly different, courage is the result of a lifestyle that has embraced knowledge in the arena it finds itself. (Note: The issue is not merely the possession of knowledge, but embracing it to the point of it producing something of worth that stands the test of time).

A good example of courage is exemplified in none other than Jesus. He goes to the cross; the cross does not come to Him. The distance between Him and the cross was that of pain and immense suffering. He envisioned the cruel blows to His body; the rejection, the agony of what it would be like under the pressure of carrying sin's burden for a lost ungrateful world. Imagine the ridicule from the creatures that He created! He knew that. He understood what He was going to suffer. It was even prophesied way before His emerging on the scene (see Isaiah 61 vs.1-2; Isaiah 53 vs.1-12). The Bible declares that His prayer of agony before His death caused Him to sweat "...as it were great drops of blood falling down to the ground." (Luke 22 verse 44 KJV). Such was the agony that He 'conceived' of the cruel crushing He was about to undertake. Yet, He went ahead, all the way to the cross and beyond. He understood the ramification of not going all the way for lost mankind, which would have resulted in a catastrophic culmination of events, towards a hell-bound eternity for humanity.

"He understood the ramification of not going all the way for lost mankind, which would have resulted in a catastrophic culmination of events, towards a hell-bound eternity for humanity."

Jesus' hour had come and He knew He had a choice. Without choice an action is under coercion, and therefore, cannot be considered courageous. This reminds me of a story told of a man who risked his life. There was a contest that promised one million dollars for anyone who could jump into a swampy area filled with crocodiles and find his or her way to the other side about a quarter of a mile away. A man is seen suddenly launching himself energetically into the warm gross water. He does so before the announcer finishes stating the rules of the contest, and finds himself scrambling franticly to the other side. No one had ever done this before! A record was now created! However, when questioned as to how he could have been so brave, the man tries to catch his breath. Astonished at his cash reward, he tells the onlookers that in an attempt to escape a hired assassin's contract put out on his life, he decided his only choice was to swim through the muddy swamp. He was at the right place at the right time. He did not even know that the swamp contained crocodiles! His action won him the prize. This man's action was not knowledge based, and therefore, cannot be considered courageous. His human instinct was in action. Jesus, however, understood the ramification, the depth of agony, the cruel crushing He would have to endure; and yet He went to the cross. No man epitomizes courage to the degree that Jesus did. He is our example.

The bravest are surely those who have the dearest vision of what is before them, glory and danger alike, and yet notwithstanding go out to meet it.[2]

Jesus' courage indeed was a by-product of His understanding of hell and eternal damnation for a lost world; and His love motivated Him to go all the way for us. As can be seen from the example of Jesus, the lifestyle of courage does not mean that we will not feel a bit reluctant or frail to go ahead, rather, in the face of all obstacles that we see or anticipate we strive to advance ahead anyway. It is not a feeling it is a decision!

"Be strong and of a good courage: for unto this people shalt thou divide for an inheritance the land, which I sware unto their fathers to give them." — Joshua 1 vs.6.

Joshua was to be courageous because of others. Vision is others focused and the verse above clearly demonstrates this truth.

The demand by God on Joshua to be of courage was backed by a promise. Besides this, Joshua was a man of understanding; he walked with Moses and saw the miracles that proceeded from his ministry, yet he also understood the kind of hard-headed people he was inheriting after Moses' departure. Despite this understanding, he answered the call. That is courage! Therefore, Joshua had some kind of understanding as the basis for his courage. People act rashly when they presume and act, instead of acting out of understanding.

Joshua 10 verse 25 KJV reads, **"...fear not, nor be dismayed, be strong and of good courage: for this shall the**

Lord do to all your enemies against whom ye fight."

Again the demand for courage is backed by a promise, providing a platform on which any subsequent action would be taken.

Even the disciples of Jesus are told by Him to **"...be of good cheer [take courage; be confident, certain, undaunted]! For I have overcome the world. [I have deprived it of power to harm you and have conquered it for you.]"** (John 16 verse 33, Amplified Bible). The basis for the demand to be courageous was the fact that Jesus provided His disciples with the understanding that He was in control. Without this truth revealed to them, there would be no basis for any consistency in their decision to follow Him.

The best decision-makers are those who are willing to suffer the most over their decision but retain their ability to be decisive.[3]

Paul in his shipwreck experience exhorts those on board with a divine word given to him by God's angel. **"Fear not Paul, thou must be brought before Caesar: and, lo, God hath given thee all them that sail with thee."** (Acts 27 verse 24). This information was to put everyone at ease as to the outcome; it was meant to 'en'-courage them. The prefix 'en' in the word encourage means "to cause or inspire". So Paul's message was meant to inspire courage in their hearts.

Courage is not a nominal or average term, not the norm in society. It is called courage because it defies nominal thinking. This is why courageous people never get advice from average thinkers; average or nominal thinkers will bring them back to the norm. When a rash act is committed and defended as a courageous act, the end result is repugnance. Repugnance means to be contradictory or inconsistent. Why? The reason is that, inconsistency is a by-product of a lack of understanding. A good example is Peter, the Lord's disciple. He was inconsistent in his devotion to Christ. He claimed he would stand by Jesus no matter the cost, but bailed out when the heat was turned on him. He lacked understanding of the circumstances that Jesus was about to undergo. This lack of understanding led to his inconsistency (Mark 14 verse 27-31).

Principle: It takes as much courage to submit to truth as it does to defend it.

Numbers 16 verses 1-16, 25-33 reveal Korah's presumption. He led a revolt against Moses. While his action seemed bold, it really was an obnoxious one, based on a misguided understanding. His so-called stand did not receive God's approval, because as far as God was concerned, it was not based on truth. Jude chapter 1 verse 11 sheds further light, "**...and perished in the gainsaying of Core (or Korah)."**

> *"You are only courageous when you understand the depth of implication involved in the act, and yet you choose to go ahead in spite of the odds against you."*

The word gainsaying comes from the Greek word antilogia, meaning to contradict. Korah's actions, though appearing bold, were not courageous. They were not based on true knowledge, but were presumptuous to the 'core.' What he set out to prove was catastrophically disproved. You are not courageous because of a daring act. You are only courageous when you understand the depth of implication involved in the act, and yet you choose to go ahead in spite of the odds against you.

Marriage is not a courageous step if knowledge is unavailable. Jumping into a commitment without knowledge of its ramification or implications is rash. Commitment based on knowledge and understanding is one based on courage. The degree of courage exercised consistently is determined by the degree of understanding acquired. So "**...in all your getting, get understanding**" (Proverbs 4 verse 7 NKJV).

THE FEARFUL STEWARD

Strangely, the expounders of many of the great new ideas of history were frequently considered on the lunatic fringe for some or all of their lives. If one stands up and is counted, from time to time one may get knocked down. But remember this: a man flattened by an opponent can get up again. A man flattened by conformity stays down for good.

—Thomas J. Watson, Jr.[4]

This is a very noble statement. We may fail in many things, but we must never fail ultimately by refusing to try again. The truth about courage and its lack thereof is further conveyed in Matthew 25 verses 14-30. The story highlights four main characters: (I) The Master. (II) The three servants. The Bible says the master gave talents (a particular kind of currency of Bible days) to his servants "according" to their individual abilities.

It is safe to conclude from Matthew 25 verses 14-25, that the Master had an understanding of the gifts, talents, and abilities of his servants, otherwise he could not have conclusively made a distinction of their differing levels of ability. Notice that the Master did not distribute to them equally. To one he gave five talents, then to the other two, and to the third servant he gave one. However, each man was given equal time (see Matthew 25 verse 19). So to rephrase the statement above we can say that he distributed to each, different portions, but the same quantity of time. It was now left to the three servants to apply themselves with what they were given.

Please take note, for them to be productive they must have known like their Master, the inherent abilities they possessed. The two servants possessing five and two talents respectively went out and used what they had. The Bible says that they "traded" (Matthew 25 verse 16). To 'trade' is to toil or labor for; it comes from the Greek word ergazomai, the root word which means energy. So these two servants exerted energy to multiply what they were given.

> *"Fear conceals our potential by paralyzing it!"*

The third servant however, hid his talent, for he was "afraid." What is fascinating is the word translated afraid connotes a sense of awe or reverence that leads to a sense of paralysis (Matthew 25 verse 25). The word 'hid' means to conceal or keep secret. Fear conceals our potential by paralyzing it!

He who loses wealth loses much; he who loses a friend loses more; but he who loses his courage loses all.[5]

So for this servant the deciding factor was fear. This man lacked the understanding of the value of his potential and so did nothing. Sad to say, there are many like this servant who bury their gifts, talents, and abilities because of fear of the unknown. This fear disables them from stepping out on the edge. Maintaining their current status is more convenient than exploring greater heights and depths of what is already theirs. They forfeit their contribution to the good of mankind.

Being positive is part of being a hero--maybe the hardest part, because if you are a hero you're smart enough to know all the reasons why you should be discouraged.[6]

Words can never adequately convey the

incredible impact of our attitude toward life. The longer I live the more convinced I become that life is 10 percent what happens to us and 90 percent how we respond to it.[7]

I remember an incident that happened nearly twenty years ago, after my brother and I finished pharmacy school. Everyone close to us knew that we were very scarce, always spending time in the library, many times twenty-five hours a week. Yet, at the completion of our pharmacy program, we sensed the need to attend Bible school; we also had an idea of which one to attend. It was clear to us that, if we did not act fast, the calling of God that we individually sensed on our lives nearly three decade ago would become aborted. Needless to say, our decision though right to us, was not a popular decision, as extended family and friends of the family questioned our decision. Some said to my mother, "They just finished a program in pharmacy, and now they are going into theology? I cannot believe it!" If not for each other, and an understanding of what God was doing with us, this opposition would have crippled our decision in seeking what God had in store for us.

The truth is that often discouragement sets in when things that happen to us do not conform to our desires or preconceived ideas. A disappointment or setback often is seen as a way to excuse ourselves of trying again. Never confuse your experience with your self-worth. You are worth more than your experience.

> *"Never confuse your experience with your self-worth. You are worth more than your experience."*

The book has not been closed on our abilities, because we have God the Almighty backing us up. **"If God be for us, who can be against us?"** (Roman 8 verses 31). Well, we can come against ourselves. Self-defeat is more devastating than any other kind. When all of God's resources say that you can, but you conclude that you cannot, you leave no room for action.

In Summary

Principle 1: An act of Courage does not necessarily make a person courageous.

Principle 2: Courage is a by-product of a deep-rooted understanding.

Principle 3: You are only courageous when you understand the depth of implication involved in the act, and yet you choose to go ahead in spite of the odds against you.

CHAPTER 30

HOW TO KEEP YOUR VISION ALIVE

"People seldom improve when they have no other model but themselves to copy."

— Oliver Goldsmith (1730-1774)

Father: Pater (in Greek) from root signifying "a nourisher, protector, upholder." (Vine's Complete Expository Dictionary).

Vine's Dictionary sheds light on the word 'Pater': Metaphorically, of the originator of a family or company of persons *animated by the same spirit as himself, as of Abraham* (Romans 4:11, 12, 16-18).

Visionaries are like fathers. A father is supposed to nourish, protect, and uphold his family. The same is true of the vision that God gives you. It must be nourished, protected, and upheld.

Three Cardinal Functions of a Visionary

1. **To nourish**: it means to feed or to be a source of supply. (See Luke 11:11-13).

The vision God has given you must be fed with the study of the Word, prayer and focus.

Joshua 1: 8: **"This book of the law shall not depart out of thy mouth; but thou shalt meditate therein day and night, that thou mayest observe to do according to all that is written therein: for then thou shalt make thy way prosperous, and then thou shalt have good success."**

Proverbs 4: 26: **"Ponder the path of thy feet, and let all thy ways be established."**

2. **A protector**: (one who guards and guides as steward over his offspring).

Nehemiah had a vision to rebuild the walls of Jerusalem. While he was conscious of the task, he was not naive regarding the capability of his enemies. With one hand they built the wall and with the other they held a weapon.

Nehemiah 4:17-20 (AMP):

"Those who built the wall and those who bore burdens loaded themselves so that everyone worked with one hand and held a weapon with the other hand, And every builder had his sword girded by his side, and so worked. And he who sounded the trumpet was at my side. And I said to the nobles and officials and the rest of the people, The work is great and scattered, and we are separated on the wall, one far from another. In whatever place you hear the sound of the trumpet, rally to us there. Our God will fight for us.

"The name of the Lord is a strong tower; the righteous run to it and are safe." Proverbs 18:10, NIV

3. **An upholder**: is one who builds esteem, inspires and sustains. In Hebrews 1:3, Jesus upholds "...all things by the word of his power..."

To uphold something means to esteem it; our visions

must be esteemed in order for others to take us seriously and make the desired impact.

Romans chapter 11, verse 13 AMP:

"But now I am speaking to you who are Gentiles. Inasmuch then as I am an apostle to the Gentiles, I lay great stress on my ministry and magnify my office."

Paul did not wait for others to stress the importance of his ministry or magnify it before others. He took responsibility for showing others the importance of his assignment.

With God's help, it is your primary responsibility to nourish, protect, and uphold the vision God gave you.

In Summary

Principle 1: The vision that God gave you must be nourished, protected, and upheld.

Principle 2: It is your primary responsibility to nourish, protect, and uphold your God given vision.

CHAPTER 31
GOD'S VISION AND PURPOSE FOR NATIONS

And He made from one [common origin, one source, one blood] all nations of men to settle on the face of the earth, having definitely determined [their] allotted periods of time and the fixed boundaries of their habitation (their settlements, lands, and abodes), So that they should seek God, in the hope that they might feel after Him and find Him, although He is not far from each one of us. For in Him we live and move and have our being; as even some of your [own] poets have said, For we are also His offspring.

(Acts 17:26-28 AMP)

God had a definite purpose in mind when He designed and orchestrated the formation of nations. In fact, you will find in Genesis that God was the grand architect of the formation of nations.

It is important to note that regardless of what nation you are from, God has a plan for your life.

Genesis, chapter 10, verse 5 (KJV) reads, **"By these were the isles of the Gentiles**

> *"It is important to note that regardless of what nation you are from, God has a plan for your life."*

divided in their lands; every one after his tongue, after their families, in their nations."

Notice here that there is no mention of race but language. The division was based on language and family. The Bible never mentions race in this passage.

This is the first mention of the word "nations" in the entire Bible. It's taken from the Hebrew word goy (pronounced gowy - see Strong's Concordance number 1471), which means 'massing', that is, a mass of people gathered together. In Genesis, the Hebrew word 'goy' is translated seventeen times as 'nations', nine times in the singular form 'nation' and one time it is translated 'Gentiles.' Could this possibly be by accident? I don't think so. From the very beginning, God had nations or all people in mind.

According to Strong's Concordance this word is often used in the Old Testament to describe Gentile nations (distinct from Israel).

Genesis chapter 10, verse 20, NIV says, **"These are the sons of Ham by their clans and languages, in their territories and nations."** Verse 31 – **"These are the sons of Shem by their clans and languages, in their territories and nations."** It is clear that the word "nations" is used repetitively.

In verse 32 we read **"These are the clans of Noah's sons, according to their lines of descent, within their nations. From these the nations spread out over the earth after the flood."**

The Power of a Single Language

Genesis, chapter 11, verses 1 to 4 AMP explains why nations were formed. It reads:

"And the whole earth was of one language and of one

accent and mode of expression. And as they journeyed eastward, they found a plain (valley) in the land of Shinar, and they settled and dwelt there. And they said one to another, Come, let us make bricks and burn them thoroughly. So they had brick for stone, and slime (bitumen) for mortar. And they said, Come, let us build us a city and a tower whose top reaches into the sky, and let us make a name for ourselves, lest we be scattered over the whole earth."

What was God's intention in Genesis, chapter 1? God told Adam and Eve: "Be fruitful, and multiply, and replenish the earth..." (Genesis 1:28 KJV). He wanted them to spread over the earth, but somehow these people got the idea that God's plan wasn't the way they wanted to live their

> *"Ambition is self-focused. Their intention was to make a name for themselves. So obviously, God was not in it."*

lives. They said, "Let's make a name for ourselves." They were ambitious. Ambition is self-focused. Their intention was to make a name for themselves. So obviously, God was not in it.

Look at God's response to their ambitious enterprise:

Genesis 11:5-6 Amplified Bible (AMP)

"And the Lord came down to see the city and the tower which the sons of men had built. And the Lord said, Behold, they are one people and they have [a]all one language; and this is only the beginning of what they will do, and now nothing they have imagined they can do will be impossible for them."

Footnote:

a. Genesis 11:6 Some noted philologists have declared

that a common origin of all languages cannot be denied. One, Max Mueller (The Science of Language), said "We have examined all possible forms which language can assume, and now we ask, can we reconcile with these three distinct forms, the radical, the terminational, the inflectional, the admission of one common origin of human speech? I answer decidedly, 'Yes'." The New Bible Commentary says, "The original unity of human language, though still far from demonstrable, becomes increasingly probable."

- Reference: Biblegateway.com

Now, what does God do in Genesis chapter 11, verses 7 through 9? **"Come, let Us go down and there confound (mix up, confuse) their language, that they may not understand one another's speech. So the Lord scattered them abroad from that place upon the face of the whole earth: and they gave up building the city. Therefore the name of it was called Babel—because there the Lord confounded the language of all the earth; and from that place the Lord scattered them abroad upon the face of the whole earth."**

"God does not believe in unity at any cost if that unity is contrary to His plan and purposes."

What do we see in this passage? We see that God established languages by confusing these people in order to disrupt their plan. God disrupted their plan by diversifying their language. Obviously God does not believe in unity at any cost if that unity is contrary to His plan and purposes.

Facts we may derive from Genesis chapter 11:

• Communication is the currency for advancement.

• Diverse languages are man's burden.

• Diverse languages are a creation of consequence. This means that these diverse languages directly correlate to what God 'saw' about where mankind was heading - So He intervened to halt this ambitious enterprise.

• God is willing to put an end to unity when it is rooted in a wrong ideology.

• With God, it is never unity at any cost.

The Burden of Diverse Languages

It is clear from this incident (at the Tower of Babel) that communication is the currency for advancement. That's why God had to confuse their language to break up their communication, to halt this ungodly enterprise. The moment their languages were mixed up confusion set in. They probably became suspicious of one another's motives when they heard a language they could not understand.

Today, diverse languages have become man's burden. Diverse languages were a creation of consequence. The disruption of this plan did not disrupt the plan of God, it preserved it. God never loses sight of the big picture. This was simply one of God's strategies to preserve man until the coming of Christ.

According to linguisticsociety.org:

"According to one count, 6,703 separate languages were spoken in the world in 1996. Of these, 1000 were spoken in the Americas, 2011 in Africa, 225 in Europe, 2165 in Asia, and 1320 in the Pacific, including Australia. These numbers should be taken with a grain of salt, because our information about many languages is scant or outdated, and it is hard to draw the line between languages and dialects. But most linguists agree that there are well over 5,000 languages in the world. A century from now, however,

many of these languages may be extinct. Some linguists believe the number may decrease by half; some say the total could fall to mere hundreds as the majority of the world's languages - most spoken by a few thousand people or less - give way to languages like English, Spanish, Portuguese, Mandarin Chinese, Russian, Indonesian, Arabic, Swahili, and Hindi. By some estimates, 80% of the world's languages may vanish within the next century."[1]

There are many difficulties in distinguishing some languages because of various dialects within a language. It is interesting to note that linguists have credited Christian missionaries with greatly helping to account for the number of languages that exist in the world today:

"Much pioneering work in documenting the languages of the world has been done by missionary organizations (such as the Summer Institute of Linguistics, now known as SIL International) with an interest in translating the Christian Bible. As of 2009, at least a portion of the bible had been translated into 2,508 different languages, still a long way short of full coverage. The most extensive catalog of the world's languages, generally taken to be as authoritative as any, is that of Ethnologue (published by SIL International), whose detailed classified list as of 2009 included 6,909 distinct languages."[2]

So in some odd sense, every time we hear a different language it should remind us of Genesis 11 and God's redemptive revelation.

Blessed to be a Blessing

In Genesis, chapter 12, and verse 2 NIV God said to Abram: **"I will make you into a great nation, and I will bless** you; I will make your name great, and you will be a blessing."

What was God's purpose for making Abram a great nation and blessing him? Answer: to be a blessing. God's plan has never changed.

Verse 3 – "...and all peoples on earth will be blessed through you."

Joseph's Redemptive Revelation of God

Joseph interpreted Pharaoh's dream and predicted seven years of plenty and another seven years of famine. God gave Joseph wisdom to give counsel to Pharaoh about what must be done to mitigate the difficult times that were ahead. He told Pharaoh to store up in the seven years of plenty so that they could be sustained adequately during the seven years of famine. The powerful thing here is, not only did Egypt have relief but so did other nations who came to buy grain from Egypt.

Genesis 41:53-57 (AMP):

"When the seven years of plenty were ended in the land of Egypt, The seven years of scarcity and famine began to come, as Joseph had said they would; the famine was in all [the surrounding] lands, but in all of Egypt there was food. But when all the land of Egypt was weakened with hunger, the people [there] cried to Pharaoh for food; and Pharaoh said to [them] all, Go to Joseph; what he says to you, do. When the famine was over all the land, Joseph opened all the storehouses and sold to the Egyptians; for the famine grew extremely distressing in the land of Egypt. And all countries came to Egypt to Joseph to buy grain, because the famine was severe over all [the known] earth."

THE VISION GUIDED LIFE

This scripture shows that Joseph is a type of Christ; it shows that God had the whole world in mind when he gave Joseph insight into the impending famine.

Verse 56 – **"When the famine was over all the land, Joseph opened all the storehouses and sold to the Egyptians, for the famine grew extremely distressing in the land of Egypt."**

Verse 57 – **"And all countries came to Egypt to Joseph to buy grain, because the famine was severe over all the known earth."**

God used Joseph as a preserver. Joseph was a type of Jesus. His dream was a redemptive revelation. Joseph possessed insight, foresight, and wisdom.

Called to Disciple Nations

After His resurrection Jesus addressed His disciples in Matthew, chapter 28, verse 18 through 20 (NIV):

"Then Jesus came to them and said, "All authority in heaven and on earth has been given to me. Therefore go and make disciples of all nations, baptizing them in the name of the Father and of the Son and of the Holy Spirit, and teaching them to obey everything I have commanded you. And surely I am with you always, to the very end of the age."

God had the world in mind. He had the nations in mind. If God has nations in mind and that is the mission He has given to us, then that's the mission we must embrace. We are here to make disciples of all nations. This is our Kingdom mandate.

Now, remember this also, when Jesus was talking to His disciples, they had a certain frame of reference, a certain mindset. Other nations were a foreign concept to them but not to

God. God had to expand their horizon.

Our mission is not through until Jesus comes.

Though the multiplicity of languages became man's burden, languages are not an obstacle for God.

Acts Chapter 2 verses 1 to 11 Young's Literal Translation (YLT) says:

"And in the day of the Pentecost being fulfilled, they were all with one accord at the same place, and there came suddenly out of the heaven a sound as of a bearing violent breath, and it filled all the house where they were sitting, and there appeared to them divided tongues, as it were of fire; it sat also upon each one of them, and they were all filled with the Holy Spirit, and began to speak with other tongues, according as the Spirit was giving them to declare. And there were dwelling in Jerusalem Jews, devout men from every nation of those under the heaven, and the rumour of this having come, the multitude came together, and was confounded, because they were each one hearing them speaking in his proper dialect, and they were all amazed, and did wonder, saying one unto another, `Lo, are not all these who are speaking Galileans? and how do we hear, each in our proper dialect, in which we were born? Parthians, and Medes, and Elamites, and those dwelling in Mesopotamia, in Judea also, and Cappadocia, Pontus, and Asia, Phrygia also, and Pamphylia, Egypt, and the parts of Libya, that [are] along Cyrene, and the strangers of Rome, both Jews and proselytes, Cretes and Arabians, we did hear them speaking in our tongues the great things of God.'

After the resurrection of Jesus, the first message

of salvation was preached on a day that every nation was represented; this goes to show that God never loses sight of the big picture. It's interesting that in Genesis, chapter 11, we see that God confuses the languages, and in Acts, chapter 2, God speaks to all the nations present despite the various languages spoken. The diverse languages were not an obstacle because God supernaturally spoke through His disciples.

One of the things that God did with the early Church is first, He told them to stay in Jerusalem until they be endued with power from on high. And after that, they were instructed to preach the gospel in Jerusalem, Judea, Samaria, and to the uttermost parts of the earth (Acts 1:8). Jerusalem was a hostile place to be. It was outside the walls of Jerusalem that Jesus was crucified at a place called Golgotha. These men took a great risk by staying in Jerusalem. But they obeyed the Lord's command. As some of the disciples experienced great persecution, they were scattered, and went throughout Judea and Samaria preaching the gospel (Acts 8:1-4). Today we are in the "uttermost" part of the world phase in God's Kingdom agenda. God's vision is being fulfilled.

Cluster Culture: The Church's Paradox

I personally know of large congregations who are raising men and women very effectively for the work of the ministry. They are equipping and sending stations. They have planted churches and built Bible schools locally and abroad.

The Mega Church is valuable and relevant for various reasons:

1. Ability to do things quickly and on a grander scale because of available resources.

2. Ability to engage and have strong relationships with its surrounding community.

3. Ability to spread the gospel more effectively by using

media and technology.

Ephesians 4:11-14 (NLT):

"Now these are the gifts Christ gave to the church: the apostles, the prophets, the evangelists, and the pastors and teachers. Their responsibility is to equip God's people to do his work and build up the church, the body of Christ. This will continue until we all come to such unity in our faith and knowledge of God's Son that we will be mature in the Lord, measuring up to the full and complete standard of Christ. Then we will no longer be immature like children. We won't be tossed and blown about by every wind of new teaching. We will not be influenced when people try to trick us with lies so clever they sound like the truth."

Consider this: some churches today, particularly the large and "successful" ones, in some ways are both innovative and in other ways have an aspect that could be viewed as primitive. The innovative part is obvious, such as the use of technology to reach the masses and establishing an undeniable community presence. Yet, there exists a primitive tendency that is in part reminiscent of the Towel of Babel. The characteristic of the 'cluster culture' seen with the Tower of Babel is the desire to 'gather' rather than 'scatter'. This same trait has crept into some churches today. The unintended consequence is, rather than adequately equip people for the work of the ministry as is stated in Ephesians chapter 4 verse 12, many people feel comfortable being served while they unconsciously view their pastors as 'performers' and themselves as 'spectators'.

The work of the ministry spoken about in Ephesians 4 is not talking about becoming a church volunteer (a form of housekeeping). The intent of this passage is our maturity and the ability to spread the gospel message as we **"...occupy till [Christ] returns."** (Luke 19:13).

Some years ago I was invited to speak to a small group of ministers. As I sat down before being introduced, my host brought up the topic of big churches (he has about 5,000 members). He asked the small group of ministers why they wanted to "have a big church". One answer particularly stood out. This minister replied as he chuckled: "So I can feel good". I was stunned. To make matters worse, I had already prepared to speak on Luke chapter 14:25-27.

Luke 14:25-27 reads:

"And there went great multitudes with him: and he turned, and said unto them, If any man come to me, and hate not his father, and mother, and wife, and children, and brethren, and sisters, yea, and his own life also, he cannot be my disciple. And whosoever doth not bear his cross, and come after me, cannot be my disciple."

I stood up and read the above scripture and emphasized the fact that though this was a large crowd following Jesus, He stressed discipleship. He delivered a hard message that few could bear. After my brief message, the silence that followed was deafening.

The Test

Are we equipping people for the work of the ministry? Are they becoming mature in Christ? Ephesians 4 is our guide. This is the test for every church.

Tower of Babel

"....The name given to the tower which the primitive fathers of our race built in the land of Shinar after the Deluge (Gen. 11:1-9). Their object in building this tower was probably that it might be seen as a rallying-point in the extensive plain of Shinar, to which they had emigrated from the uplands of

Armenia, and so prevent their being scattered abroad. But God interposed and defeated their design by confounding their language, and hence the name Babel, meaning "confusion." In the Babylonian tablets there is an account of this event, and also of the creation and the deluge."[3]

According to churchleaders.com:

"Less than 20% of Americans regularly attend church...Olson, director of church planting for the Evangelical Covenant Church (covchurch.org), began collecting data in the late "80s, gradually expanding his research to encompass overall attendance trends in the Church. In his study, he tracked the annual attendance of more than 200,000 individual Orthodox Christian churches (the accepted U.S. church universe is 330,000). To determine attendance at the remaining 100,000-plus Orthodox Christian churches, he used statistical models, which included multiplying a church's membership number by the denomination's membership-to-attendance ratio."[4]

So while we have more churches today - and many more mega churches than ever before, actual regular church attendance is less than twenty-percent. This means we have a lot more ground to cover to effectively impact our culture.

Power of Ideology

A working definition of the word ideology: a formed belief that governs our actions.

Ideologies are powerful - so powerful that God "...**came down to see the city and the tower which the sons of men had built.**" (Genesis 11:5).

The Tower of Babel shows us that opposing ideologies cannot coexist without finding common ground. Jesus spoke of

the incompatibility of "New wine in old wineskins" in Matthew
9:17. You must exchange one ideology for another or find a
common ground that both parties can agree on.

Peter Learns a Big Lesson

Unfortunately Peter's ideology did not allow him to
see salvation in Christ beyond the Jewish people. Peter's first
message was to only the Jews:

Acts 2: 5 **"And there were dwelling at Jerusalem Jews,
devout men, out of every nation under heaven."**

On the day of Pentecost it wasn't quickly apparent that
Peter was in his comfort zone in so far as he was preaching to
people of his own Jewish-ethnic heritage. Peter had to learn
the hard way that Jesus was for both Jew and Gentile. Peter's
teachable moment had fully come when he was sent by God to
preach the gospel to a Gentile named Cornelius.

ACTS 10: 25-28, KJV:

**"And as Peter was coming in, Cornelius met him,
and fell down at his feet, and worshipped him. But
Peter took him up, saying, Stand up; I myself also am
a man. And as he talked with him, he went in, and
found many that were come together. And he said
unto them, Ye know how that it is an unlawful thing
for a man that is a Jew to keep company, or come
unto one of another nation; but God hath shewed me
that I should not call any man common or unclean."**

Some scholars estimate that the time of this encounter
in Acts chapter 10, the Church was eight to ten years old. This
means that Peter struggled with this ideology of the exclusion of
Gentiles or non-Jews from the gospel of the Kingdom, about a
decade after the day of Pentecost.

We must realize that we have to see the mission of Christ in a non-ethnic way (a Bible-based ideology). There is a possibility to be a missionary in another country and only target your 'own' people who also migrated from your country of origin. Our presence in a foreign land can only penetrate the culture if we extend our reach beyond our ethnic boundaries.

Peter: Two Levels of Progressive Revelation

1. Level one: It took a divine revelation to show Peter that the Gentiles are not unclean. The passage below is underlined for emphasis:

Acts chapter 10, verse 28 (AMP):

"And he said to them, You yourselves are aware how it is not lawful or permissible for a Jew to keep company with or to visit or [even] to come near or to speak first to anyone of another nationality, but God has shown and taught me by words that I should not call any human being common or unhallowed or [ceremonially] unclean."

2. Level two: Peter learns that God has no favorites. This step goes beyond level one. That is, it is one thing to no longer believe that the Gentiles are common or unclean; but it is quite a bigger deal for a Jew to utter an admission that God has no favorites after centuries of observing such a well-established ideology among the Jews. The passage below is underlined for emphasis:

Acts chapter 10, verse 34-35 (AMP):

"And Peter opened his mouth and said: Most certainly and thoroughly I now perceive and understand that God shows no partiality and is no respecter of persons, But in every nation he who venerates and has a reverential fear for God, treating

Him with worshipful obedience and living uprightly, is acceptable to Him and sure of being received and welcomed [by Him]."

The End brings us back to the Beginning

God shows us in Revelation what He saw from the beginning; here we gain a glimpse into how the end will turn out. The end brings us back to God's original intent. Despite the fall of man, time (past or present), and all the events that have shaped our world, one thing is certain, God has never lost sight of the big picture. He has kept His eyes on the ball.

Revelations 7: 9-12 (AMP):

"After this I looked and a vast host appeared which no one could count, [gathered out] of every nation, from all tribes and peoples and languages. These stood before the throne and before the Lamb; they were attired in white robes, with palm branches in their hands. In loud voice they cried, saying, [Our] salvation is due to our God, Who is seated on the throne, and to the Lamb [to Them we owe our deliverance]! And all the angels were standing round the throne and round the elders [of the heavenly Sanhedrin] and the four living creatures, and they fell prostrate before the throne and worshiped God. Amen! (So be it!) they cried. Blessing and glory and majesty and splendor and wisdom and thanks and honor and power and might [be ascribed] to our God to the ages and ages (forever and ever, throughout the eternities of the eternities)! Amen! (So be it!)"

God cannot be stranded. He cannot be held hostage to man's shortcomings. In the end, out of every nation, tribe and people and language His purpose will be fulfilled.

Find Your Place and Fulfill Your Purpose

Given the enormous plan of God, we cannot afford to minimize our role in God's agenda. We are all vital to His plan.

"Now you [collectively] are Christ's body and [individually] you are members of it, each part severally and distinct [each with his own place and function]."(1 Corinthians 12: 27 AMP).

The effectiveness of the body of Christ is subject to the effectiveness of each member functioning in his or her individual role. The more mature we are individually, the more effective we are poised to be as ambassadors of Christ (collectively).

Five Things about You that were Predetermined

It is safe to say that there are at least five things you had no control over that pertains to your entry into this earth.

1. Where you were born

Where you were born speaks of the geographical location of your birth. Your birth place was without your consent.

2. The Conditions under which you were born

If your parents were wealthy, poor, or middle class, your birth was impacted by your parents' condition or status. Whether privileged or impoverished, you had no control over the conditions under which you came into the world.

3. Who Your Parents were

You did not choose your parents. This is a reality. You and I were introduced to our parents as helpless babies. You inherited the ethnicity of your parents and that ethnicity cannot be changed.

4. Your Gender at Birth

While later in life people have found ways to "alter" their gender, a person's gender at birth was predetermined by God.

5. When You were Born

This speaks of the 'time in history' of your birth; you did not decide to be born in this time in history. This is a very significant but obvious fact we must swallow. No amount of wishing can alter this fact.

The great news is that your purpose lies in the generation in which God has placed you.

"And He ...having definitely determined [their] allotted periods of time..." (Acts 17:26 AMP).

None of us is here by accident. Our presence on earth at this time in history was predetermined by God.

There is however one thing you do have control over: who you become in life. This is true of every individual, family, business, and nation. This is one thing you can do something about.

In Summary

Principle 1: God had a definite purpose in mind when He designed and orchestrated the formation of nations.

Principle 2: Today, diverse languages have become man's burden.

Principle 3: Communication is the currency for advancement.

Principle 4: Diverse languages are a creation of consequence.

Principle 5: God is not hindered by languages.

Principle 6: We have been called to disciple nations.

Principle 7: God will bring all nations under one umbrella, the Lordship of Jesus.

SECTION VII
STATE YOUR LIFE'S MISSION

CHAPTER 32

HOW TO WRITE A COMPELLING MISSION STATEMENT

My Uncle Joe used to tell me that during World War II if an unidentified soldier appeared suddenly behind the lines and could not state his mission, he was automatically shot without question. That is clarity with an exclamation point! The real point here is that your mission is a living and real part of who you are. It is not something you do one time so you can say you have a mission statement. It actually becomes the way you live life... When you live your mission, the blurred images align and you can determine if you are on the right path.

—Laurie Beth Jones, author, *The Path*

The Apostle John left no room for guessing when it came to the mission of Jesus, when he stated in the latter part of 1st John, chapter 3, verse 8: **For this purpose the Son of God was manifested, that He might destroy the works of the devil.** Like Jesus, it is imperative that we know and are able to articulate our mission with clarity.

In the beginning of Jesus' ministry He walked into the synagogue and made an unforgettable reading from the book of Isaiah. In Luke 4:18-21 [NIV] we read these powerful words of Jesus' mission statement:

"The Spirit of the Lord is on me, because he has anointed me to proclaim good news to the poor. He has sent me to proclaim freedom for the prisoners and recovery of sight for the blind, to set the oppressed free, to proclaim the year of the Lord's favor." Then he rolled up the scroll, gave it back to the attendant and sat down. The eyes of everyone in the synagogue were fastened on him. He began by saying to them, "Today this scripture is fulfilled in your hearing."

Jesus changed the way this scripture would be seen or heard forever. He told His hearers that He was the one Isaiah talked about. To all that heard Him, the implication was clear. They knew that this scripture was a snapshot of the Messiah's mission.

One of the most effective communicators of the gospel was unquestionably the Apostle Paul. The man could not be silenced, stopped, or intimidated. He was a man on a mission and he knew what his mission was. In several places Paul made it crystal clear why he was alive. Every waking moment of his life was for a singular purpose. Look at the following statements by Paul:

Paul wanted to know Christ at all cost:

Philippians 3:10, 11 NKJV

"that I may know Him and the power of His resurrection, and the fellowship of His sufferings, being conformed to His death, if, by any means, I may attain to the resurrection from the dead."

Paul wanted to make Christ known:

Colossians 1:28 NKJV

"Him we preach, warning every man and teaching every man in all wisdom, that we may present every man perfect in Christ Jesus."

1 Corinthians 9:22, 23 NIV

"To the weak I became weak, to win the weak. I have become all things to all people so that by all possible means I might save some. I do all this for the sake of the gospel, that I may share in its blessings."

Romans 1:5, 6 NIV

"Through him we received grace and apostleship to call all the Gentiles to the obedience that comes from faith for his name's sake. And you also are among those Gentiles who are called to belong to Jesus Christ."

Paul wanted to make Christ known regardless of the circumstance:

Acts 20:21-24 NKJV

"testifying to Jews, and also to Greeks, repentance toward God and faith toward our Lord Jesus Christ. And see, now I go bound in the spirit to Jerusalem, not knowing the things that will happen to me there, except that the Holy Spirit testifies in every city, saying that chains and tribulations await me. But none of these things move me; nor do I count my life dear to myself, so that I may finish my race with joy, and the ministry which I received from the Lord Jesus, to testify to the gospel of the grace of God."

Since Paul clearly knew his mission, he also knew when he had accomplished it. Close to the end of his life he makes this declaration in 2 Timothy 4:6, 7 [KJV]: **"For I am now ready to be offered, and the time of my departure is at hand. I have fought a good fight, I have finished my course, I have kept the faith:"**

"It is hard to state a mission you do not know. It is equally hard to motivate others to live a mission you cannot state."

It is hard to state a mission you do not know. It is equally hard to motivate others to live a mission you cannot state.

A compelling Mission Statement is important for the individual, church, ministry, business, and, family.

A mission statement is a statement of the purpose of [an]...organization or person.... A mission statement answers the question, "Why do we exist?"[1]

To motivate others, it is important that you clearly articulate a statement of your mission that is both compelling and inspiring.

A Mission Statement should have the following qualities:

1. It must convey the purpose you want to achieve in the simplest and clearest way.

2. It should provoke readers or listeners to action. Habakkuk 2:2 (AMP):

"And the Lord answered me and said, Write the vision and engrave it so plainly upon tablets that

everyone who passes may [be able to] read [it easily and quickly] as he hastens by."

3. It must be *aggressive* (meaning that it must be "marked by combative readiness" – Merriam-Webster Dictionary). The words *combative readiness* sound very much like military terminology. This means a compelling Mission Statement should do the same thing that a soldier's orders accomplish; that is, the statement must be proactive and have an 'active' rather than a passive voice or tone.

4. It should be written so succinctly that others can memorize it in whole or at least remember key parts of the statement in order to take personal ownership of it.

"Only convey words that make sense and are straight to the point."

5. Avoid using words that are vague in meaning. There is nothing more annoying to people than gibberish or nonsensical word pictures. Only convey words that make sense and are straight to the point.

According to Joanne Fritz, Ph.D., who specializes in nonprofit organizations, there are five things to avoid in a Mission Statement:

1. Jargon that only professionals in your particular field will understand.

2. Stilted, formal language.

3. Passive voice (passive: "xyz is an organization that helps women achieve independence"; active: "xyz helps women achieve independence.")

4. A focus on the organization, rather than the people it serves.

5. Generalities, such as "saving the world" or "eradicating poverty."

Sometimes a Mission Statement fails in its objective because it lacks certain key elements. You could say that there is a science to a compelling well-written Mission Statement.

There are Three Components of a Compelling Mission Statement:[2]

I. Purpose Statement: Why does your organization exist? What is the purpose you exist to achieve? This is the foundational question to a compelling mission statement. Once you have determined this part move to the next components below.

II. Business Statement: This part of your mission statement addresses how you intend to fulfill your purpose. This part gives readers or listeners a window into your strategy. Remember John 3:16; God's strategy was giving Jesus. Many times the business statement can be identified by what follows the word 'through' or 'by.' The word 'through' or 'by' points to your method.

III. Value Statement: This component focuses on what particular core values drive your purpose.

CASE STUDIES

Case study #1

God's 'Mission Statement':

John 3:16 (AMP):

"For God so greatly loved and dearly prized the world that He [even] gave up His only begotten (unique) Son, so that

whoever believes in (trusts in, clings to, relies on) Him shall not perish (come to destruction, be lost) but have eternal (everlasting) life."

Let's examine God's Mission Statement to identify the three components we've learned.

I. Value Statement:

What motivated God's action?

- Love: *"For God so greatly loved and dearly prized the world..."*

- Eternal life: *".... have eternal (everlasting) life."*

II. Business Statement:

God's method or strategy to bring salvation to mankind:

- *".... gave up His only begotten (unique) Son..."*

III. Purpose Statement:

Why He sent His Son?

- *".... so that whoever believes in (trusts in, clings to, relies on) Him shall not perish (come to destruction, be lost) but have eternal (everlasting) life."*

Case study #2

The Mission Statement of Vision for Life Ministries:

To train, equip, motivate, and empower men and women for successful living through image building, identity, vision, and purpose based ministry; to the end that the individual will realize the significance of his or her individuality, gain a positive picture of his or her God-given destiny, resulting in self discovery and a maximized life for Kingdom advancement in society and the world at large.

Let's examine our Mission Statement to identify the three components we've learned.

I. Purpose Statement:

"To train, equip, motivate, and empower men and women for successful living..."

II. Business Statement:

"...through image building, identity, vision, and purpose based ministry...."

III. Value Statement:

"...gain a positive picture of his or her God-given destiny, resulting in self discovery and a maximized life for Kingdom advancement in society and the world at large."

The Exercise:

1. Try to write three separate statements using the three components above. Tweak each statement as much as possible to clearly convey what you want readers to know about you or your organization.

2. Merge the three statements into one sentence or short paragraph in a way that makes sense.

Now practice here:

I. My Purpose Statement (reason you exist):

_____

_____

_____

II. My Business Statement (strategy):

_____
_____
_____
_____
_____
_____
_____
_____
_____

III. Value Statement (core values):

_____
_____
_____
_____
_____
_____
_____

Finally, merge the three components into one statement

(Your Mission Statement):

_____
_____
_____
_____

28 DAY GROUP
EXERCISE

FIRST WEEK:

DAY 1 THROUGH DAY 7

It is important as you start this group discussion that you create a positive environment. You may open up in prayer first. If you have eight or more people you can divide into groups. Then you can encourage each person within the group to introduce him or herself. You could also open with some worship. If you are leading the group discussions, play the role of a facilitator not expert. None of us has arrived. Make sure that you are vulnerable to the group in areas that you still struggle. Note: you do not have to follow these questions religiously. You can improvise or add questions of your own. Try to encourage each person in the group to participate.

Sections I and II Group Questions:

1. Why is Proverbs 29 verse 18 important to the discussion on Vision?

2. Is being a leader a substitute for Vision? Explain your answer.

3. Where do you look to identify if a Vision is present? Explain your answer.

4. Do you agree with this statement? "Vision is not purpose." Explain your answer.

5. Can you know your Purpose and still lack Vision?

6. Is Vision a plan for the unexpected or is it deliberate? Explain.

7. If you had to choose one which would you rather have: Vision or Charisma?

8. How is Reputation different from Vision?

9. What is the difference between Ambition and Vision? Give examples.

10. What happens when a Program becomes a substitute for Vision?

11. Are all Dreamers visionaries? Explain your answer.

NOTES

_____

_____

_____

_____

_____

_____

_____

_____

_____

_____

_____

_____

_____

_____

_____

SECOND WEEK:

DAY 8 THROUGH DAY 14

Section III and IV Group Questions:

1. Is God's kingdom a kingdom of superstars? Explain your answer.

2. What question(s) do you have about the subject of Vision?

3. What is Vision from God's point of view?

4. What does "Vision sees the outcome" mean?

5. Name the two powerful concepts that make up Vision?

6. What did Joseph learn about his "Visions"?

7. What New Testament scripture(s) reveal God's redemptive revelation?

8. How can a Vision be obtained? Please list them and explain each one.

    a._____

    b._____

    c._____

d._____

NOTES

_____

_____

_____

_____

_____

_____

_____

_____

_____

_____

_____

_____

_____

_____

_____

_____

_____

_____

_____

_____

_____

_____

_____

_____

_____

_____

_____

_____

_____

THIRD WEEK:

DAY 15 THROUGH DAY 21

Section V Group Questions:

1. What does Vision 'restrains us' mean?

2. How does Vision create structure?

3. How can Vision create stability and order? Give some real life examples.

4. How does Vision create motivation? Explain your answer.

5. What else does Vision do to a person? Explain.

NOTES

_____

_____

_____

_____

_____

_____

_____

_____

_____

_____

FOURTH WEEK:

DAY 22 THROUGH DAY 28

Section VI to VII Group Questions:

1. What is God's Mission Statement?

2. A complete Mission Statement has how many components? Name and explain each one

    a._____

    b._____

    c._____

3. What was Nehemiah's assignment?

4. Do you know your assignment?

5. To what length should we go to fulfill our assignment?

6. Can there be two standards of Excellence? Please explain.

7. Explain the Pot roast analogy. What do you understand by this analogy?

8. Should we ask questions or just follow traditions at face value?

9. What do you understand by the Forerunner Principle? Give examples of forerunners.

10. How should we respond to obstacles as we pursue our God-given vision? Explain.

11. What is courage?

12. Is courage the absence of the feeling of fear? Explain.

13. What does it mean to nourish, protect, and uphold your God-given vision? Explain briefly.

14. What led to the creation of nations? Is God concerned about nations? Explain.

15. Do you know how to write a compelling Mission statement? Can you state it succinctly?

NOTES

_____
_____
_____
_____
_____
_____
_____
_____
_____
_____
_____
_____
_____
_____

TURNING POINT

Your decision will affect your:
- Present
- Destiny
- Family
- Peace of Mind
- Eternity

There are some truths you need to know right now:
1. God loves you.
2. Sin separates you from God.
3. Jesus died for your sins.
4. You can be saved by believing in Jesus and confessing Him as your LORD and Savior.

Receive the Lord Jesus Christ today!

Your Decision

"If you confess with your mouth the Lord Jesus and believe in your heart that God has raised Him from the dead, you will be saved." Romans 10:9

Pray this prayer from your heart:

Dear Lord, I accept the gift of eternal life today. I acknowledge that I am a sinner in need of salvation. Thank you for sending your Son, Jesus, into the world to die for me. Jesus, I confess you as my personal Lord and Savior, and I believe that you were raised from the dead. Come into my life and make me a new creature.

For free literature to help you in your relationship with God write to:
Vision For Life Ministries
P.O.Box 3553
Broken Arrow, Oklahoma
74013

NOTES

1. Chapter 1

1. Enjoy Life Club, Vol. 7, No. 4, October 1991.

2. 6000 Plus Illustrations for Communicating Biblical Truths: A Man Who Possesses Grandeur.

3. The Law of the Lid, The 21 Irrefutable Laws of Leadership By John C. Maxwell.

4. Source Air Power Study Center. www.fas.org.

2. Chapter 3

1. 6000 Plus Illustrations for Communicating Biblical Truths: Christopher Columbus.

2. M. Hirsh Goldberg, The Blunder Book, (Quill, 1984), pp. 151-152.

3. Chapter 5

1. Chapter 136. Illustrations Unlimited, Wisdom: First Priority

4. Chapter 6

1. Easton's Bible Dictionary, in the Bible Scholar App for Smart phones & Tablets.

2. Illustrations Unlimited: Point of View: Different Mentalities, Chapter 11.

3. Chapter 111 Illustrations Unlimited: Point of View: Can you top this?

5. Chapter 7

1. Illustrations Unlimited: Talk, Chapter 129.

6. Chapter 9

1. 6000 Plus Illustrations for Communicating Biblical Truths: Great Dreams.

7. Chapter 11

1 . Illustrations Unlimited, Chapter 111 Point of View: Finding What We are looking for.

8. Chapter 13

1. James S. Hewitt, Illustrations Unlimited (Wheaton: Tyndale House Publishers, Inc, 1988) , 244-45.

9. Chapter 14

1. The Blunder Book, (Quill, 1984), p. 151.

10. Chapter 15

1. Fr. John Powell in "Through Seasons of the Heart".

Christianity Today, Vol. 33, no. 14.

2.   Outcome, Method and Resource based on US Army Organization Effectiveness Center, Ft Ord, California.

3.   James S. Hewett, Illustrations Unlimited (Wheaton: Tyndale House Publishers, Inc. 1988) p. 156.

11. Chapter 16

1. The Success Journey, (Nelson, 1997), p. 39.

12. Chapter 22

1. www.fhwa.dot.gov/ohim/onh00/onh2p9.htm

13. Chapter 24

1. Illustrations Unlimited (Chapter 111, Point of View: Basic Vision)

14. Chapter 27

1. Encyclopedia Britannica on William Wilberforce

2. Thomas J. Stanley, Ph.D., The Millionaire Mind (Kansas City: Andrews McMeel Publishing, 2000), 19-20.

15. Chapter 28

1. Unknown, Leadership, Vol. 4, no. 1.

2. James S. Hewitt, Illustrations Unlimited (Wheaton: Tyndale House Publishers, Inc, 1988), 19-20.

16. Chapter 29

1. Theodore Roosevelt, Leadership, Vol.15, no. 3.

2. Thucydides, Leadership, Vol. 15, no. 3.

3. M. Scott Peck. Leadership, Vol. 15, no. 3.

4. Thomas J. Watson, Jr., Chairman of Board, IBM, Leadership, Vol. 1, no.1.

5. Miguel de Cervantes, Spanish author, 16th century. Men of Integrity, Vol. 1, no. 1.

6. Michael Doris. Leadership, Vol. 16, no. 4.

7. Charles R. Swindoll, Christian Reader, Vol. 33, no. 4.

17. Chapter 31

1. http://www.linguisticsociety.org/content/what-endangered-language

2. http://www.linguisticsociety.org/content/how-many-languages-are-there-world

3. Easton's Bible Dictionary, in the Bible Scholar App for Smartphones & Tablets.

4. http://www.churchleaders.com/pastors/pastor-articles/139575-7-startling-facts-an-up-close-look-at-church-attendance-in-america.html

18. Chapter 32

1. Wikipedia on mission statements

2. www.nccsdataweb.urban.org on non-profit organizations.

Invite the Taiwos to Your Event!

Olu Taiwo, BSc., DPh.
FOUNDER

Kay Taiwo, BSc., DPh.
FOUNDER

About the Taiwos, founders of
Vision for Life Ministries, International.

Identical twins, Kay and Olu Taiwo are international speakers, ministers, consultants, featured authors, and licensed Pharmacists. With over 20 years of speaking experience, their ministry has impacted audiences in Ukraine, Nigeria, England, Philippines, Zimbabwe, South Africa, Canada and across the USA.

To invite the Taiwos to speak at your church, conference or event, write to:
VFLM, Inc. P.O. Box 3553 Broken Arrow, OK 74013 or
Please visit their website: www.vflm.org.

Made in the USA
Las Vegas, NV
25 August 2021

28852008R00116